upon THE PEARL the crown

eight cantos

ROSÉ

eight cantos

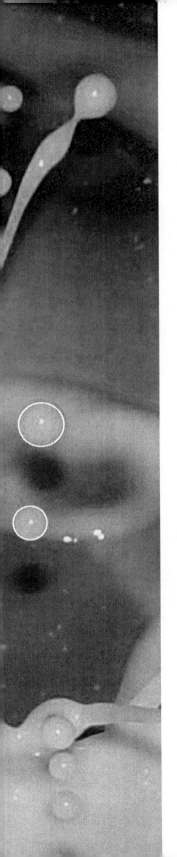

THE PEARL upon the crown

To a Friend of Paul's

Rosé

ROSÉ

SYNERGETIC PRESS
SANTA FE, NEW MEXICO 2012

Published by SYNERGETIC PRESS
1 Bluebird Court, Santa Fe, NM 87508

Library of Congress
Cataloging-in-Publication Data

Rosé, 1934-
  The pearl upon the crown : eight cantos / by Rosé.
      p. cm.
  ISBN 978-0-907791-41-6
  I. Title.
  PS3618.O7826P43 2012
  811`.6—dc22

                              2011021206

BOOK DESIGN: Arlyn Eve Nathan
EDITOR: Linda Sperling
TYPESETTING: Aurelia Gale
PRINTING: Lightning Source

PHOTOGRAPH FOR COVER & INTERIOR © by Dror Bar-Natan

contents

Preface

The Pearl Upon the Crown is a thirty year on-going sometimes mock-heroic, sometimes heroic epic poem. Somewhere in the middle of 1978 I wrote two stanzas in my notebook and then immediately forgot them until two years later. In June of 1980 while delving through my notes I came across them again. I read them aloud a few times then continued writing in the same six-line stanza form until the Muse and I decided we had come to the end.

There were a hundred stanzas. I was bubbling with ideas and raring to go. By the mid 1980s I had written five 100 stanza cantos in rhymed, metered verse, in iambic tetrameter with a rhyme scheme of AAX BBX

> *Hey hombre! I remember when*
> *A string bag cost a couple yen*
> *Up the Chamula Road*
> *And I could buy, back in my youth*
> *For just a buck, at the subway booth*
> *A twenty token load*

Searching for a title for this epic that was pouring out of me I came across a haunting image: one drop of milk falling into a bowl of milk. As the drop lands a ring, a circlet, a crown with five or six points rises up from the bowl of milk with the drop now hovering above the center of the crown–*The Pearl Upon the Crown*.

For the next decade and a half I wrote lots of poetry and although I thought of The Pearl often and jotted down notes and lines and rhymes I did little writing of the epic. In early 2001 both the Muse and I were ready. The new millennium switched me to an eight line stanza, a favorite of the great Italian renaissance epic poets, the *ottava rima*, also used in the magnificent mock heroic epic *Don Juan* by Lord Byron. This stanza is in iambic pentameter with the concluding couplet usually in hexameter. The rhyme scheme is AB AB AB XX

> *Sometimes I dream I'm dancing with the flowers*
> *Their willow slimness folded in my arms*
> *We whirl about in summer thundershowers*
> *Their leaves, caressing gently, fill my palms*
> *And I might steal a kiss beneath the bowers*
> *And they kiss back without the slightest qualms*
> *Their petals with exquisite softness brush my lips*
> *And we embrace as pollen flies and nectar drips*

Still in 100 stanza, cantos but running twice as long as the earlier ones, The Pearl now added three more cantos to itself.

As of publication of the Eight Cantos in 2011 I am halfway through Canto Nine which I expect to finish, along with who knows how many other cantos in this lifetime or the next.

— ROSÉ

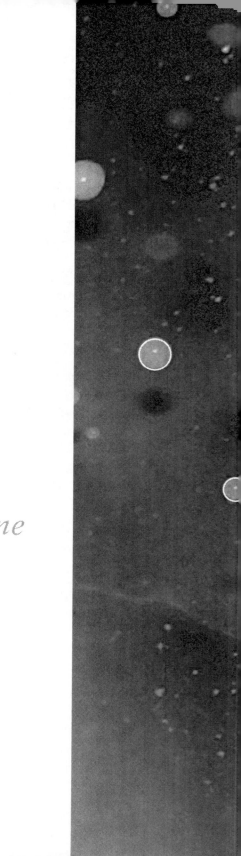

canto one

TROPIC

Hey hombre! I remember when
A string bag cost a couple yen
Up the Chamula Road
And I could buy, back in my youth
For just a buck, at the subway booth
A twenty token load

But now the world stands on its end —
Since flexibility means bend
To shake the heavy snows
I brave a Florida that's hot
Humidity and jungle rot
And sand between the toes

I wander in the blazing heat
Where Cubans shuffle down the street
And yellowed palm trees strive
With concrete forests steely blue
And smoke-ring gaseous exhaust stew
To barely stay alive.

And in a tiny coffee shop —
More stand or counter — stool spin stop
I drink the expressed bean
In a toy cup there's half a shot
It's concentrated on the spot
Liquid amphetamine!

And mighty as the Cubans are
In love, in battle, in their car —
No matter what they do
Only a few cups can they down
Within the day, or surely drown
In that exotic brew

Believe me then with much amaze
The Cubans stared and fixed their gaze
On me and on my friend
When several times a day we'd drink
Three triples straight, without a blink
O that Cubano blend!

Well fortified with that hot mud
The tiny bubbles in my blood
All singing the same tune
I motor to the Panda Bar
Along the ghetto's open scar
The dark side of the moon

Race-riot ringers line the walls
And leap from ambush-eaten halls
To range the thoroughfares
That teenage rebel's camo suit
Has sewn-in pockets stuffed with loot
And room for poison flares

A dozen blocks of sun-drenched slum
Half floating in the puddled rum
Are empty now at dawn
Emerging from this quaint mirage
Sleek limousines in the garage
Sport cycles on the lawn

And here at morning's quiet hour
With all drapes drawn against the power
Of the relentless sun
The Panda Bar erupts in sin,
And all the multi-colored skin
Slowly begins to run

Abstract albinos weave their way
Through rows of pimps in lilac spray
And high-crowned Western hats
Hoodlums in jackets with a bulge
Informers ready to divulge
More pimps in shades and spats

A famous entertainer sips
Black Russians through her famous lips
White powder on her nose
Ceremonial hookers flash
Outrageous limbs and ritual gash
Sweat damp and musky rose

The master of the perfect scam,
The trickster, con, the on-the-lam,
The flake, the shark, the pro —
High-rollers on the skids, on bail,
Mere interlopers out of jail
Are toasting toe to toe

The bar is jammed with criss-cross legs,
Silk suits, boiled shirts — the cream, the dregs
Rehearse the night's mayhem
And coiled in the leather booths
Snake ladies tell half-lies, half-truths —
It's only nine A.M.

While in the perfect dark, the throb
Of every heart as some poor slob
Is goosed by a movie star
The morning crowd is getting tight
They all thank God it's still last night
Inside the Panda Bar

But now it's time to cut them loose
To find myself fresh orange juice
Squeezed right before my eyes
In tropic Florida — a snap
On every corner there's a tap
Of O.J. from the skies

But like so many tales you're told
Where streets — whole towns are paved with gold
And money grows on trees
You rarely find the thing you seek
Fresh-squeezed means earlier that week
They bring you to your knees

Let's off to see the salt-sand reach
Of fabulous Miami Beach
The Pearl upon the Crown —
Immaculate uncluttered sweep
Of crashing waves and ocean deep
Will never let you down

I saw it from the plane but found
A different story on the ground
For all the brochures say
Through heat in which an egg could fry
Humidity? There's nothing dry
I drove for half a day

At last I learned what no one knew —
The beach is there, the ocean blue
You just need X-ray eyes
The view is blocked at every stop
To see the beach you'd have to chop
The hotels down to size

Yes, twenty miles and only twice
I caught a glimpse, a tiny slice
　　Of serviceable shore
A pocket beach, a meager ledge,
All else hotels from end to edge
　　From floor to marble floor

And yet the beach a bonus brought —
I was the only living sport
　　To frolic on the sands
For all the tourists all the fools
Were packed into the swimming pools
　　While working on their tans

For lunch I stroll the avenues
The ancient stronghold of the Jews
　　Smoked salmon on a tray —
I'm Jewish — on my parents' side
So I enjoy the crimson tide
　　Of borscht in Biscayne Bay

I play the horses, play the dogs
Hit all the air-conditioned morgues,
　　Nightspots along the strip
A sail, a dive, a fish or two —
There must be something else to do
　　Miami is so hip!

I know! I've seen a dozen chaps
Who keep their business under wraps
Executive-type trash
Men about town, well groomed, discreet,
Who sweep a lady off her feet
And always pay in cash

What do they do? Their wallets show
No papers — they're as clean as snow
Their eyes like diamond drills
The kind of guy who's never stopped
Although his bag is always topped
With hundred dollar bills

I know Miami is the scene
I've seen it on the silver screen
I've even seen the Grove —
Its arty fairs and private clubs
Its fancy shops and tricky pubs
Where minor painters strove

If minor artists are a jest
One hundred fifty miles southwest
Might be a place to go
Two major pushers of the pen
Used to hang out there now and then
Before things got too slow

Strange how both put themselves away
The poet on a morning gray
Stepped off the cruising ship
The storyteller had his fun
He turned around his favorite gun
And let his finger slip

Their songs are stilled, Ernest and Hart
One in the deeps — the leaden dart
The other has brought down
They both knew the tropic horror
Now they're worn on Fame's tiara
Two Pearls upon the Crown

So don't allow the gallant South
To press his lips upon your mouth
His teeth to touch your throat
Florida's a land of bubbles —
If you don't have any troubles
Then get yourself a goat

Or see the Everglades, my friend
You'll never need a swamp again
After that sea of grass —
The anacondas love it there
And fruit bats settle in your hair
Mosquitoes up the ass!

I must admit the necklace Keys
Strung emeralds in the turquoise seas
A steel-spanned jeweled toad
Is startling when the sun's just right —
But mostly it's the dead of night
When driving down that road

Despite swamp, sweat, secretions vile
There's something makes it all worthwhile
Despite scimitar sun
A miracle beyond belief —
It's sailing for the coral reef
Out on a long day's run

Down two dozen feet — protrusions
Fairytale coral confusions
Rise from the ocean floor
Moving weightless with the motion
Of the undulating ocean
Green grottos we explore

In every hole, nook, cranny, space
Through fissure, hollow, rainbows race
Like darting color wheels
In every cave a grouper waits —
While amberjacks move after mates
We're swimming past like seals

Each vision, color, texture, grain
Stags horn, elks horn, starburst, brain
Is mottled, speckled, wrought
Into fantastic lava flows —
The living coral slowly grows —
Architecture of thought

Between the patches of the reef
Marauders swarm in high relief
Dangerous doctors dire
They operate without a splash
It's vivisection when they flash
Teeth of surgical fire

And coming at us, looking wrong
A pearl-gray suit quite twelve feet long
A kind of dreadful tux —
With belly white and formal tails
This socialite always prevails —
A Hammerhead De Luxe!

He circles, spirals, flips a fin
Veers erratically moving in —
Stops, to adjust his tie —
He seems so elegant and slim
A fellow gentleman — to him
We're sandwiches on rye

Perhaps it's not yet time for lunch
For joining with another bunch
Of diners on the go —
The Hammerhead pays his respects
Although he never pays the checks
For dinner or the show

This calm, this crystal clear serene
Breathtaking underwater dream
Of sea anemones
Is so profound that we forgot
Our breath is held — Beneath the yacht
We're rising by degrees

To surface on the lesser world
Where banners wave and hair is curled
A world of "makin' bucks"
Where every day some rotten penny
Will ask you if "you're gettin' any"
Where life's a game of knucks

Those precious hours underneath
Will linger while you brush your teeth
Only your senses drown
To leave the chamber of the seas
Like leaving distant galaxies
A long ride back to town

But what is time? Do you defend
The theory that time has no end?
Like numbers infinite
The days draw on and to the sum
A scholar needs to add but one
One little tiny bit.

To prove beyond a doubt his pet
Hypothesis, he'll take a jet
To the earth's very core
When all the time we'll never know —
A curtain closes our brief show
And we can see no more

For some — although we're growing older —
Time's in the eye of the beholder
Like love. They'll name a spot
Say punctuality's their rule —
And I'll be there like some poor fool
At seven on the dot

May all such scoundrels poorly thrive!
For when they finally arrive
They think they're right on time
And if I point out that our date
Was hours ago — "Is it that late?
Is that an awful crime?"

"My watch was slow, I fell asleep
I got this phone call from some creep —
I merely missed the train
See this hole where my foot got caught!
It was for half past ten I thought,
I've so much on my brain"

"But what's the fuss? At any rate
There's one thing sure, I'm never late —
Just look, I've ruined my socks!"
That's right! They'll saunter by at ten
And say that perfect gentlemen
Are never bound by clocks

By all that's holy I declare
By all the pagan gods, I swear
I'll live to see him hung
Who dares once more to make me wait
Who even comes one minute late
After the bell has rung!

Time who is so vast and airy
Time who's just a little scary
When marooned or such —
Time whose passage knows no borders
Time whose movements stump recorders
Whose trained eyes don't miss much

Time is a mighty paradox
Well hidden, like a Chinese box
From every casual eye —
Time is an unfolding saga
Playing us a morning raga
On strings that seem to sigh

When young, an hour takes all day
To pass — Each minute seems to stay
Life's an eternal theme —
But now that time is running out
How can you for a moment doubt
That life is but a dream?

A dream is odd — for what appears
As several hours or several years
To dreamers lost in sleep
Is nothing quite so long at all
The time elapsed is very small
The time our watches keep

So several days in dreams have passed
While scientists observe the fast
Flutterings of our lids
A journey to the middle earth
They tell us, was five seconds worth —
Proved by lines on their grids

My thoughts are coming in profusions!
Are dreams just one of time's illusions?
It really makes you think!
After that ride back from the reef
Perhaps the most ideal relief
Would be a good stiff drink

Or better yet, let's have a feast
And drink the mythological beast
Kirin Beer and sake —
Served up with a gigantic dish
Of raw delicious fresh-sliced fish
By the sushi jockey

Now here's the only food that works!
For while a hundred million jerks
Are dining out on beef
Those fellows with the almond eyes
Have planned another sea-surprise
Fresh from the coral reef

Imagine, if you can, a cake
Elaborate as a man can bake
With towers, spires, flags
A floating island in the breeze
With every topping you can squeeze
Until the table sags

Yet so composed that if you took
One piece away, a different look
     Entirely, this dish
Would then present. How can we eat
You ask, half of this monstrous sweet
     Don't fret— it's all raw fish!

Yes, this rosette is salmon pale
Arranged between some yellow-tail
     That orange splash is roe
Do they eat like this on Luna?
King clam, octopus and tuna
     Tied with a seaweed bow

Red snapper is sliced paper thin
Pink abalone, dark blue fin
     Bay scallops stuffed in nests
Of snails and eels— and to my shame
Some purple item I can't name —
     Let's dine, my honored guests

Food for thought — a worthy trade —
     You cannot be much better paid
     For thinking than with fish —
Now for example, way back when
I heard a tale more Hebrew Zen
     Than anything you'd wish

A celebrated simpleton
Who searched the world and finding none
Of all the things he sought
Asked a Jewish gentleman —
Or was it a monk from Japan?
If knowledge could be bought

He asked why Jews — or Nipponese —
Were just as smart as you could please
The answer: "Herring heads —
For just a couple bucks a throw
You'll be completely in the know
You'll lecture to the Feds"

So, every day this chap would pop
Into the oriental shop
Buy fish heads from the Jew
Until one day he stopped to think
Poised upon enlightenment's brink
He thought he really knew

He raced across town to the store
The Yiddish Jap stood by the door —
"How come I pay two bucks
For herring heads? Am I so dense?
The whole fish costs just fifty cents!
Are we goy sitting ducks?"

Inscrutable, the Jews — the Japs —
Known for never caught taking naps
The answer came out steady:
"Hold on, my friend, I'm not a crook
The money is not lost, just look!
You're getting smarter already"

A simple tale for pleasure told
To pass the time while growing old
Some words to plug the gap
A story's made to fill the crunch
Between — devouring late brunch —
And the afternoon nap

A mere diversion, fancy flights
Witness the Thousand And One Nights
A literary vat!
Magic words all cares may banish
Words that while they're spoken vanish
But nothing more than that

A story cannot buy you food —
Unless, of course, it change the mood
Of melancholy King
Then the reward is dancing girls
Who'll stuff your mouth with antique pearls
To praise the song you sing

An ancient custom, very rare
That's practiced to maintain the glare
Of spotlights on the throne
Magnificent the King who throws
Loose pearls into the mouths of those
Who sing instead of groan

From out your mouth they tumble down
Enough to set upon a crown
And several dozen more
Perfect spheres of iridescence
Lucent globes of oyster essence
They roll upon the floor

The melancholy King admits
He's free completely now from fits
Of melancholia —
Hysterically, he helps retrieve
A giant pearl, I do believe
That's from Mongolia

And hands it to you with the rest
Of all the other pearls, the best —
"Eat this and make a wish!
Just pop it down and don't be rude
Although we know it is not food
At least, we're sure it's fish!"

Don't hold your breath or wait too long
For often you can sing a song
Or tell a splendid tale
And wait all year for your reward
Till pearls into your mouth are poured
Like golden sparkling ale

A tale is just a pleasantry
That circulates like currency
Along the boulevards
It's not as if you heard a myth —
A legendary romance with
Asides from famous bards

There's not much worth remembering —
Dissection or dismembering
Makes nothing very bright
A bagatelle — a mere vignetta
Hardly worth a small vendetta
Or the poor candle-light

Burnt in the telling of the tale —
The stuff that's in the morning mail
Will pass the time as well
Just as long as it's amusing
And there's nothing more confusing
Than a glass of Muscatel —

Unless you believe what Sufis say
How just a tale can change the way
You looked at things before —
The course you followed all your life
Your home, your family, your wife
The many vows you swore

Can in an instant disappear
Replaced by such a vision clear —
Such a terrible light —
It borders on insanity
Your friends will think it's vanity
They watch you stride the night

Transfigured utterly beyond
The pale and insubstantial bond
That never lets us speak —
You walk on air crowned with glory
Just because you heard a story
Accidentally, last week

The Japanese invented Zen
To clear the minds of mortal men
From superfluity —
With just one line of a Koan
They'll serve you up enlightened man —
And no gratuity

So when I speak of herring heads
There's something there beyond the threads
With which a tale is spun —
With every layer that is peeled
Another meaning is revealed
And then a deeper one —

Ad-infinitum — to the end —
The meanings and the layers blend
And somehow from this mix
Despite the matter and the mirth
Or maybe — from their union — birth
A tiny flame that licks

Into the corners of your mind
The wheels that used to merely grind
Are fired into life —
Along the chakra serpentine
A metamorphosis divine
A flashing crystal knife

You are transformed, you are the lock —
Now, more important things than hock
And a soda water
Are your concerns — the tale was key
To your unfulfilled destiny —
You were ripe for slaughter

Even before that tale was stilled
All that's inside of you was killed
And made over anew
The cells aligned, the circuits jumped
All of your former features trumped
And there were quite a few

It is as if you spent your whole
Life searching for some unknown goal
You were suffocating —
Now, thrown by random circumstance
Into the story-tellers' trance
There is no more waiting

You have emerged from a cocoon
A chrysalis — the great monsoon
Has swept your being clean —
Surrounding air is filled with sparks
With laser light and countless quarks
With energy unseen

There is no doubt you are a man
Reborn, remade, whose mind can span
Limits of time and place
Through the fabric interstitial
You are making your initial
Grand voyage into space

While hordes of well-wishers wish you
Luck, and dab their eyes with tissue
Your life becomes unbound
To their astonishment complete
They see — but can't believe — your feet
Are rising off the ground!

Well, you can fast for forty days
Or contemplate a Chinese vase
Or raise your arms above
Your head and hold them there all year
Till visions come and disappear
Or concentrate on love

Or prayers, or deeds — the blessed kind
Suspend the functions of your mind
In amniotic tanks
Or practice varied magic arts
Probe deep into your heart of hearts
And simply draw blanks

Or try yogic postures, tantric twists
Enveloping yourself in mists
Of marijuana smoke
All are effective to a point —
Right now I'm lighting up a joint
And hoping I don't choke

On special diets, sleepless nights —
The ancient rituals and rites
The thousand different modes
Designed to elevate the soul
To bring it nearer to its goal
Before — the thing corrodes

Becomes a rusted entity
A thing without identity
There's hardly any chance
A breakthrough will occur before
You turn into a total boor
And need an ambulance

To rush you from the scene to spare
Your friends from having mal-de-mer
And not even a pill
To save them from that awful motion —
When you get stuck on some new notion
Why, everyone gets ill!

So just relax and take a bath —
There is a way to find the path —
To open up the door
Remember this, someway, somehow
Things are more like they are right now
Than they ever were before!

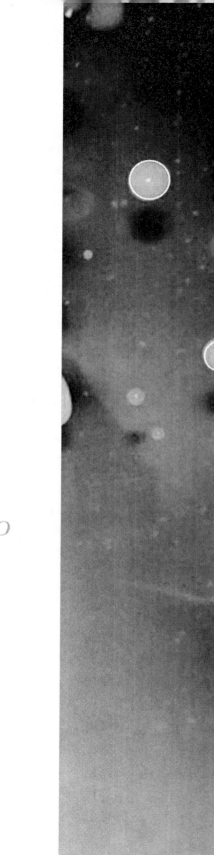

canto two

FAMOUS UNKNOWNS

I used to hang around those spots
Frequented most by polyglots
And lounge on Persian rugs
I'd only smoke the stuff or sniff
Because it made me feel as if
I didn't need no drugs!

Now, after you've said: "polyglot"
There's very little you cannot
Say and make them swallow —
Even that double negative
Sounds fashionably decorative
Or does it ring hollow?

I also tried exotic girls
I learned from mistresses of Earls
After a brief encounter
The only way to show a lass
That you are smoother, brighter, fas-
Ter is to straightway mount her

In fact, I spent a lot of time
Between the verses and the rhyme
Outright womanizing.
I found those legs, those thighs, those hips
Eurasian and Venusian lips
Much too appetizing

To ever think I had enough
I'd lie around all day en buff
In some palatial suite
The Hotel Mons, the Hotel Loins
And stroke the lovely ladies' groins
Rosette and Marguerite,

Ramona, Eunice, Babs and Flo —
Girls from the archipelago!
A sister of two queens
A pair of twins who knew the ropes
(Gazelles among the antelopes)
And several dozen teens

I never needed a translator
To speak to girls from the Equator
The Andes or the Rhine
If niceties we need distinguish
I'd talk away in body English
There was a Florentine...

A Duchess, I remember now
We met upon the strand somehow
She turned her head real quick!
Her gown was lapis lazuli
She certainly was shocked when I
Performed the cigarette trick

I'd lay a lighted cigarette
Along my finger tops and let
The burning end stick out
No more than just a tiny bit
Then with the other hand I'd hit
My back-palm and I'd shout:

"I never miss" and with these words
As elegant as flights of birds
Migrating to the south
The burning cigarette would leap
(Slim acrobat aroused from sleep)
And flip into my mouth!

Take it from me it's quite a show,
You can't believe the way girls go
Into a kind of fit!
There's something 'bout a cigarette
Describing arcs that makes them sweat
And instantly submit

To flattery or a caress
Right here she's taking off her dress
It's down around her hips,
Her thighs, her legs -- with an embrace
The Duchess, in a public place
Deftly my pants unzips

They have a way, the very rich
No matter where they are, an itch
Must instantly be scratched
On the streets, in a museum
Taking pleasure, Carpe Diem!
The moment must be snatched

The Duchess certainly was no
Exception. She'd shout: "Tally-Ho"
And follow her instinct
She never thought to spare the spur
She carried on as if she were
Soon to become extinct

We danced through Florence, Rome, Milan
I took her to the Vatican
(She made me do it there)
We checked into a French Dude Ranch
She did it in an avalanche
With someone named Pierre

I'd lock my sweet Madame Moselle
Inside the suite of our hotel
I tried to insulate her
But she'd be back in bed before
I stepped outside and closed the door
With a room-service waiter!

In Sicily — the volcano —
While watching all that lava flow
One night in Syracuse
So overcome by her great thirst
She got a publisher named Hearst
To help her reproduce —

He thought — a series of novellas
But after several tarantellas
Her meaning became clear
As long as she could find a mate
She was content to fecundate
Across the hemisphere

Her appetites were strange and vast
She must have spent some time in past
Lives as a courtesan
Some royal concubine who learned
The proper way a trick is turned
For the Emperor of Japan

Or for a Sultan, an Emir
She did it strictly for the sheer
Unimaginable
Pleasure that it always brought her
She was Aphrodite's daughter
Running after trouble

Which she found at every corner
When a brutal love had torn her
Into shreds and patches
She'd crystallize into her stance
And rush out seeking high romance
At the Polo matches

She left me down in Mexico
And ran off with an Eskimo
Who came there for the races
She found it cozy on her back
When upside-down in his kayak
She'd put me through the paces

Now, Browning's Duchess had a flaw
All Duchesses I ever saw
Were prey to this defect
Including mine --- the Duke was grave
She'd smile at him and at a knave
A rose or an insect

A leper from the Hebrides
A puppy dog scratching his fleas
The same sweet smile she wore
For everyone and everything
The Duke, a messenger, a King
To each she gave no more

Or less — her eyes were always lit
Totally indiscriminate
She gave her very all
How can we say this trait's a sin?
Her love went deeper than the skin
"No fault" is what I'd call

If I were judge. But still the Duke
Had had enough to make him puke
Upon the marble floor
He didn't care that she could see
The fashioning of destiny
In the essential core

Of every creature, man or mouse
That's why her smile lit up his house
He wished that she were dead
He had a little tête-à-tête
And henchmen came to separate
Her body from her head!

I wonder what became of Bella
My Duchess, or was her name Stella?
I hope she didn't meet
The executioner's hard block
She never could have stood the shock
She was much too elite.

I left you in the tub, my friends!
While I was focusing my lens
On those erotic views
That filled the moments of my youth
If I were to reveal the truth
I still today confuse

The body with the soul. It's true!
The water's hot enough for you?
You seem to understand.
So close are spirit and the meat
That while I'm washing off your feet
My soul's kissing your hand

I'll write for you a thousand poems
Adorn your hair with tortoise combs
Your fingers with spun gold
Have carpets of expensive stuff —
Antique embroidered brocade fluff —
Before your feet unrolled

I'll dress you in a feather cape
A velvet choker round your nape
Your feet in crystal heels...
And bid the orchestra commence
Such music as deprives the sense
Until your body reels

Abandoned in a Dervish dance
A herald to the soul's advance
You shed your mortal cloak
Unsheathed, your spirit rides above
Your body like the holy dove
I tell you it's no joke

The way the spirit can range free
Why, every time you talk to me
It issues from your lips
Those soft words you've just now spoken
Are fragments of the soul unbroken
Let your eyes come to grips

With mine. I see your soul leap out
And uncontained, with piercing shout
Like those that shatter glass
It sparkles with a clarity
A vivid gem-fire rarity
I meant to stroke your ass

But quite forgot — forgot the cape
The mortal cloak — immortal shape
The rose upon your cheek
All were forgotten in the rush
When from your eyes your soul did gush
They say the flesh is weak

But I forgot your breasts, your hair
(Cascading, balustraded stair-
Way to a paradise)
Forgot the way your living skin
Glows soft and rich like old satin
With traceries of ice

Forgot those legs, those thighs, those hips
Ineluctable finger tips
Those ornaments of life
Forgot that stately Goddess walk
Why, I almost forgot to talk
Even forgot my wife.

I forgot I caught amnesia
From a beauty in Tunisia
Just worshipping her thigh
Her papers showed that she was clean
The doctors certified her scene
I can't remember why!

Forgot what gorgeous labia
Adorn girls from Arabia —
I think the way they ride
Their camels with a wrestler's grip
Develops muscles in the hip
And tickles their inside

So overwhelmed to see your essence
Sparkling with effervescence
Your naked burning soul
Emerge from out your body's door
I drop my chopsticks on the floor
Forgetting to be droll

I left you in the tub, I say —
I promise you a tale and stray
Into the Sushi bar —
So impolite — while you refresh
I confuse spirit with the flesh
They're very similar

When looked at in a certain light
This cage that holds the spirit tight
And evanescent soul
Are both imperfect models of
The Pearl upon the Crown above
The unfragmented whole

The perfect concept, pure ideal
That vision stamped in stainless steel
The Prime Engraver's plate
That strikes editions of the soul
And body — from the press they roll
Like books but animate

Book of the body, book of flesh
The spirit-form made ever fresh
A mystery so deep
No wonder that confusion reigns
For even though the soul attains
Plateaus — the flesh must creep

Unable to perform the part
Possessing neither skill nor art
Nor strength nor purpose firm
The body in its madness rambles
Leaving in its wake a shambles
For the conqueror worm

It's really quite a fix we're in
This cage, this crate of living skin
This pile of spare parts
This sleeping hunk of raddled meat
Somnambulism on two feet
Waking by fits and starts

This sink in which we yearly pour
Enough to drown a commodore
And nearly all his crew
We stuff with battleships of food
Enough to feed a multitude
A floating barbecue

This Angel form — half animal
We imitate the cannibal
So desperate to survive
Like sharks who in blood frenzy heat
Devour chunks of their own meat
We eat ourselves alive

Like bacteria introduced
To septic systems long misused
To gobble up the sludge
The food you think is passing through
Is actually eating you
If I am any judge

But have no fear that you'll expire
Decomposition's stopped by fire
And now the meal is done —
A cheroot on the veranda
Don't believe that propaganda
Smoking is really fun

Yes, even as I write this line
I'm yielding to a genuine
Never to be denied
Desire most implacable
So primal it's untrackable
A truly bona fide

Need to reach into my pockets
Twist my arms from out their sockets
If that's the only way
To get that precious pack of smokes
Into my hands, have a few pokes
Savor the rich bouquet

Of Turkish and Havana blend
Allow me, please, to recommend
That taste upon the tongue —
Tobacco — Raleigh said: "Divine"
That relaxation of the spine
And ecstasy of lung

I want to drop my fountain pen
And smoke a cigarette again
Some sweet Virginia leaf —
Can anything in life replace
That hot voluptuous embrace
The agonized relief

Of lighting up a cigarette
Positioning that minaret
Just right between the lips?
To suck the fiery mouthfuls in
To puff that smoking javelin
And feel the mild whips

Of fire dancing in your throat
There's only one known antidote —
And that's to have another!
The spiral curls of smoke erase
All memories of pain, disgrace —
In smoke I'd rather smother

Than rot away behind a desk
Become a thing half barbaresque
Deprived of my fresh pack —
Unnerved, unjubilant, unclean
Quite useless without nicotine
The thrice divine tabac

When I'm struck with a brilliant thought
I thank the Lord my carton's bought
And in the cabinet —
Just knowing that ten packs are there
Relieves the tension in the air —
I swear, a cigarette

Enhances every single act
The most mundane, the most abstract
And you can make a bet
To lend grace, enthusiasm
To avoid a daily spasm
I'll need a cigarette!

Sometimes although I puff and puff
I feel I haven't had enough
But since I'm not a dunce
I'll pull a handful from the pack
And, like a pyromaniac
Light them all up at once

So what if there's a little taste
Of mucilage, library paste
A hint of Elmer's glue?
Who cares if they're a little stale
When you are longing to inhale
They're sweet as honeydew

Far sweeter, now I think on it
I hope I never have to quit
(Like ordinary saps
Chew gum and bite my fingernails)
The kind of pleasure smoke unveils
Is made for special chaps

When Trace-Purcell was asked to stop
By members of the Club who'd hop
Upon his case all day
Rehearse the toxic side effects
Hereditary birth defects
The price he'd have to pay

For filling up his lungs with smoke
The dangers of a fatal stroke
He'd swear it smacked of theft:
"Damn funny business, old chaps
Put my tobacco under wraps
And I'll have nothing left!"

God, Ex-Commander Trace-Purcell!
We knew each other very well —
If one can know another
We saved each other's lives in spite
Of fear which makes betrayal bright-
Er than skin of blood-brother

We stuck it out through thin and thick
Depending on the lightning quick
Movements of our money
If the cash flowed to him from me
His attitude was one of glee
If not — I was in honey

One morning, hot upon the trail
Of wildebeest, he seemed to fail —
He turned and asked me if
I thought the applications of
Mustachio wax below, above
Still held his mustache stiff —

He thought it drooped a bit, perhaps
And then he started burning maps
          To get the water hot
Enough to shave, right on the track —
Wildebeest breathing down our back —
          I gave it my best shot

And held the mirror to his face
Master of the leisurely pace
          He dawdled through his shave
And I suppose that if I fell
Headfirst in quicksand, pits of Hell
          He'd just as quickly save

My life as I did his — You see,
Action, Despair and Unity's
          The motto of our Club
It's just good form and no wonder
When a member's going under
          To un-stopper the tub!

As long as there's a shred of hope
Just throw a Bwana enough rope
          And if he doesn't sprain
An ankle, break a leg — some gang
Of Sherpas from the hills will hang
          Him with it. Or a train

Will slice the worthy chap in halves
While he's admiring the calves
Of girls who're looking cool
Expeditions to the jungle
Are not the time or place to bungle —
That's a Bwana's Club rule

The last I ever saw of him
Was disappearing round the rim
Two hundred feet below
Straight downward and descending yet
Until his glowing cigarette
Was all that's left to show

But he survived, so goes the tale
Although I only saw the pale
Haggard storyteller
Reiterate that close escape
And then produce Trace's last tape
Which contained a stellar

Performance of the Bwana's creed
A list of animals that he'd
Discovered in the brush
(More mythological I'm sure
Than everyday big game that you're
Familiar with) I blush

Recounting what came next — a poem
Nay, several ones. That devilish gnome
        Was talking onto tape
    In some forgotten hidden spot
Most likely more half-dead than not
        Inspired by the grape

Or native drink with which he liked
To have his whiskey-soda spiked
        Waxing sentimental —
    Just picture it: his ranger hat
Sways in the breeze, falls to the mat
        With a sound as gentle

As unheard melodies are sweet
The man ought to be making neat
        Bundles of loose events
    Tying up ends, presenting facts
Recording views, reviewing acts
        Instead of making dents

In that fragile, polished, tender
Vehicle whose brilliant fender
        Is the King's own English —
    You'd think that those years in the bush
Had cured him of such school girl mush —
        Poetry is ticklish

In the best of circumstances —
Poets move around in trances
And wander from the trail
Yet here in some small palm-thatched hut
Our Trace-Purcell crushed out his butt
And told the final tale

In words supercharged with meaning
The test for poetry is leaning
With all your inner ear
Against the poem as it comes through —
A perfect one, out of the blue
Will make you disappear

And there it is — I ask, my friend,
Can you find a happier end?
The man realized his form
His nature, being, life, his art —
(Though penniless with a broken heart)
That image keeps him warm

Succinct and pithy — to the point —
He knew the time was out of joint
He's picking up the stub
Of some fresh stepped-on cigarette
It's raining and the streets are wet
Outside the Bwana's Club.

A quarter of a century
Has thrilled us with immensity
Since Trace-Purcell became
A member of the Bwana's Club
His former life completely scrubbed
Adopted his new name

Before the club he used to hang
Around with a musician's gang
His closest pal was Lacy
They were fellows of a kidney
Trace was Bix and Steve was Sidney
Look very hard, you may see

Their record made in fifty four
Sutton was Trace's name then, for
The book — You should have heard
That music very few could hear
Insistent, agonized and clear —
Trace was Miles — Lacy, Bird

Then shortly after Trace gave up
The trumpet, cornet, muting cup
Even the mellophone —
Stretch the fabric, nothing's giving —
There's no way to make a living
Seeking the perfect tone

But Lacy, from a different cut
Of cloth, cared nothing for the hut
    Of thatch, the trapper's cage
To wander the unbeaten tract
Was not his idea of an act
    He much preferred the stage

The public eye and public ear
Deep in the bush you cannot hear
    Contemporary sound
Except the roaring of some beast
So Lacy hung about the East
    Coast and he played around

In tiny clubs — Bowery Five-spot,
The Blue Note, Half Note — le jazz hot —
    Montmartre, Riviera —
To name a few of those quaint dives
That period in memory thrives
    New York primavera

When Hawk sat in with Al Bandini
(A mismatch like Ben Mussolini
    And Joe DiMaggio)
But nobody was finding work
Not even as a soda jerk
    No less quartet or trio

So off Lacy went to Paris
To the perpetual embarrass-
Ment of the U.S.A.
Find it strange to see a master
Of the arts who's nourished faster
A continent away

Than on his own native soil?
Our policy is not to spoil
The artist on the fringe
Remember how the Living Theater
Was hounded from the U.S. clear ta'
Europe — It makes you cringe

And then we shamefully request
Years late: "Come back, as honored guest"
And so it came about
That Lacy, an expatriate
For decades now, finds himself fit
To have another bout

In old New York (new wave and punk)
To honor and interpret Monk
For just a couple days
And suddenly by chance or choice
I'm poking through the Village Voice
And what should meet my gaze?

But an ad, an advertisement
For the general appraisement
Of every citizen
To say: Lacy et al's in town,
A string of pearls to deck the crown
Of Monk — I grab my pen

I jot the number on the wall
And after making one quick call
We're talking on the phone —
Now, twenty years have passed since I've
Seen him or heard his music strive
For mastery of tone

We talk a bit of this, of that
"A million things to do" we chat
And then I sort of sigh:
"I'm working on an epic song"
A pause, and then he says: "Sounds long"
And then we say "Goodbye"

I guess he really ought to know
For next week on the radio
A Lacy marathon
Is starting up, all set to go
It runs for NINETY hours or so...
But Lacy, he's long gone

To Paris — Day and night, it runs
While moons and stars and setting suns
Revolve throughout the sky
But Lacy, he's in Paris-town
His music tipped me upside-down
And nearly made me cry

In twenty years a lot of things
Go down and what the future brings
Is always a surprise
I think I'd rather throw my lot
With famous unknown artists, not
Commercial enterprise

With Bellavia, Price, with Trace
Art is the gnome — your life, the chase
So Lacy, let us try
To meet again sometime before
Another twenty years or more
Go plunging headlong by

And maybe we can mix it up
Invite the Muse in for a cup
And if she brings my pen
And if you play a tune right through
My words, around, between, unto —
We'll ask her in again!

So Lacy, that's what I propose —
But wait, Rosé, this canto grows
Beyond the bounds, the bend!
It must be stopped, or else like fruit
Too ripe, drop rotten at the root
Hold tight! I've got to END.

canto three

PARADISE

They ask me everywhere I go
What things are like in Mexico
"New Mexico," I say
How do you pass the time out there
In San Jose, does it compare...?
"No, No! It's Santa Fe!"

Well, we lie around all day in splendor
Ambrosia, nectar in the blender
On terraced mountain tops —
Like gods in pearl encrusted boots
We speak only in absolutes
And pull out all the stops

Hop in your car and drive out there
Stars swim in pools of crystal air
You're in for a surprise
The welcome station knows your name
They're overjoyed, so glad you came
They even know your size!

Yes, spread upon the desert lawn
Your own pearl boots, your own new sawn-
Off shotgun and for luck
Old turquoise beads, a western hat
Coors beer, string tie, a lariat
And brand new pick-up truck

They give you maps, a few stiff shots
Some priceless Pueblo Indian pots
And send you on your way
Along that road so charming, quaint
Where there's no need to feel restraint —
The trail to Santa Fe

The open skies, the endless plain
Highway rest stops that serve champagne
The cactus silhouette
That dominates the distant hills
And then without fanfare or frills
One more perfect sunset

As you go roaring down the road
But wait! That car ahead has slowed
He signals like a gent
He's pulling in, you'd better stop!
A combination litter drop
And Historic Monument

Is coming up — don't think I mock —
This grand affair, like Camel Rock
Is something you must see
Look! Ancient writing on the cliff
Stop here, my friends, especially if
You have to take a pee

It's Paradise, I won't be vague
Land of the Flea, Home of the Plague
The cozy Great Southwest —
Smart dinner clubs, Art without reason
Prison riots, the Opera Season
So different from the nest

Where I grew up deep in the Bronx
You won't find many honky-tonks
Adorning my birthplace
Composed of hills and vacant lots
Devoid of after-dinner spots
I mention this in case

You find yourself marooned up there
Breathing that clear provincial air
And wondering if you're bored
Alone, astride the great frontier
You wonder where that good Bronx cheer
You've heard about, is stored

Don't tap your guide impatiently
Demanding that he instantly
Return you to the city —
Like standing under mistletoe
You have to have some sense to know
When you're sitting pretty

Nearby there stands a house of glass
Magnificent enough to pass
All men's understanding
With palms high up in orange air
Rooms, wings, with corridors to spare
Even the most demanding

Tourist would readily admit
'Twere an asylum he'd commit
Himself without pardons —
So beautiful is this expanse!
Here's something worth a second glance
The Botanical Gardens

Look, a woman's walking down the street —
The loungers come alive and greet
Her with variety:
"Hey, baby, how's about I put
My finger on your foxy foot?"
Café Society

Cannot even hold a candle
To the special way they handle
A Barrio amour
Composed of catcalls mixed with hisses:
"Hey, baby, I just know the missus
Ain't coming back till four"

She pivots on her crazy pin —
A Vargas out of some Gershwin
Sequence of primal slaughter
On the streets — exuding sex —
Old men are polishing their specs
And spitting globs of water

"Hey Mama, Sugar, Baby Dolly
Pat your cake, eat your tamale!
Hey lover, come on back!"
She slowly turns, with royal step
She lifts her dress and shows her crêpe
Suzette: "You, eat this, Jack!"

The whole block freezes right in place!
Now, here's a chance to really lose face
By doing the wrong thing —
But the psyche undeveloped
Not prepared to be enveloped
Not quite set to bring

Imagination to the fore
When stricken at the very core
Is staggered more or less
With their hands deep in their pockets
Pictures of Mom in their lockets
They watch her hike her dress

And tuck it under at the waist
Their insides, turning now to paste
'Cause nothing's underneath —
I mean, no garment made of silk
Just peaches, cream, honey and milk —
Some fifty sets of teeth

Are clenched, a hundred eyes or so
Bulging a mile wide still grow
Least that's the way it seems
She's giving them no time to stall
She speaks: "Did I hear someone call?"
This stuff's right out of dreams!

But in their dreams these fiery youth —
Gay blades of the telephone booth —
Amidst damsels' appeals
Cut different figures altogether
In reality's stormy weather
These wimps make hopeless squeals

Rising to a situation's
Not the forte of these Haitians,
Spics, micks, wops, poles and kikes,
Primal throwbacks, genetic jinx,
Evolutionary kinks –
You're sure to see their likes

In any melting pot downtown
Pink, yellow golden, white, black, brown
Kids from Puerto Rico,
Sugar loaf head Yucatecans,
Chinese slanty-eyed Jamaicans,
Ali, Solly, Chico

And standing there beside the wall
A couple from before the fall —
Pure, but very evil
He hides a blade, she's chewing gum
Gorilla paste, spawn of the slum
Quite beyond retrieval!

When you meet them in Morocco
Pretty Susan, ethnic Paco
Somehow they're very quaint
But when they're standing at the gate —
Two years later — of your estate
You'd have to be a saint

To keep your fingers from the whistle
That bares dog's teeth and makes backs bristle
While leaping for the throat
They look like terrorists who just
Hijacked a plane, the kind you'd trust
To commandeer a boat

Of diplomats and send it down
(Or blow it up before they drown
Cause drowning is too easy)
Unless presented with a ransom
Many nations would think handsome
They're definitely sleazy

And now the crowd retires, fades
Dissolves into the alley-glades
As night begins to drop
That brazen hussy — what a lass!
Adjusts the dress about her ass
Covers her lollipop

And fixes you upon her pin
Invades the mind, she's stepping in
Demanding your attention
Dear heart of God — is that a purr?
Lips at your ear, "Good evening, Sir"
Sweet Mother of Invention! —

Explore her body and her mind
For several days — you know you'll find
Absolutely nothing
More than just the merest cover —
Go ahead and rediscover
The thousandth hollow ring

The empty trapeze of the flesh —
Go on and let your bodies mesh
Plow another fallow
Furrow. If every wall's a door
It merely proves that way down deep, you're
Really very shallow

So heave your body in that rift
To seize the meaning in the drift
Muster all your power
And concentrate it in the tip
Of your latest relationship
Or take a cold shower...

For tempering your iron will
Then jog around the park until
Your lungs have had enough —
Inhale, breathe deep, each breath is wealth
A penny in the bank of health
Let's show the world your stuff

Poets, philosophers and Kings
Minds and bodies are the same things
To a hard-working whore —
Predicting quakes, designing planes
Posting enormous karmic gains
Are all a dreadful bore

To girls who try to earn a buck
Selling the insubstantial fuck
To guys who'd rather pay
Cash on the line, one time, in front
(Before they moil and toil and grunt)
Than through the nose all day

And the romance, where has it gone?
The flowers, chocolates, the charm
All mating games exude?
The frills, the petticoats and lace
The mad excitement of the chase
The thrill of the prelude?

Don't ask me, Jack, I just work here
The Boss is out today, this year
This whole epoch maybe
He left and took the keys with him
We can't close down, adjust or trim
The sails of this baby

Romance is mush, the old song goes
No blushing brides or bashful beaux
Are found among the beasts
No celebration, no event
No ritual or sentiment
No relatives or priests

No oaths proclaimed or roses flung
No promises sworn with lying tongue
Elaborate masquerades
No run-about, no money-dig
No casting couch, no thingamajig —
Electric sexual aids!

The wilder beasts (the ones on fours)
When they're in heat remove their drawers
(No! We're the ones with pants)
They pounce, they mount and start right in
Without soft lights or violin
Or powdered irritants...

My father told me long ago
So many things that I was slow
In appreciating
His words of wisdom — down the drain
He warned me not to eat chow mein
And to stop masturbating!

So I ate plenty Chinese food
To spite his holy attitude
Because it was denied
And constantly would yank my wang —
I knew the thrill, the swoon, the pang
But neither satisfied

My appetites — they'd merely tease —
To masturbate, eat food Chinese
Those pleasures I'd pursue
Great bowls of shrimp chow mein devour
Then drop my fruitless passion flower
That's all I'd ever do!

But soon, to my complete distress
A sudden hollow emptiness
Would take me at the door
Your belly's full one minute past
And then, as if fresh from a fast
You've got to eat some more!

The same with pulling on your tool —
The photo flash is almost cruel
So transient and fleeting
One second, heaven welcomes you
Then up the creek with no canoe —
Whacking off and eating

Then wisdom pointed out the truth
I learned as I played out my youth
I might as well have eaten
The greaseburger with melted cheese
Chow mein, it seems, is as Chinese
As Einstein is a cretin!

And that affair with Damsel Hands
(As well as countless one-night stands
With every kind of mate)
Was fun, like bogus Chinese meals —
But now it's abalone, eels!
And I'm a graduate

Of certain secret sexual schools
We concentrate on molecules
Until the body faints —
Our policy is to abstain
We store our seed inside the brain
And, much like yogic saints

We never let our fluid drop
To breed a Golden Gully crop
But rather let it rise
Along the spinal circuitry
Until it nestles perfectly
Right there, behind the eyes

So both things that he warned me of
Chicken chow mein, one-handed love
Turned out empty pockets
A burst of flame, taste buds explode
Before you know you've shot your load
Pancaked, burnt-out rockets

Yes, Dad was right again, it seems
I'm glad he never forbade dreams
Because at just that time
I dreamed unto the maximum
Sweet dreams — a whole compendium
And usually in rhyme

I had a dream in Therapy
Years, years ago and it cured me —
A troop of interns held
Me — eagle spread, face down, above
My father's image like a glove
And bade our bodies meld

He wore a polo shirt in stripes
Reverting slowly to archetypes
I screamed as we came close
Lowered in that long feared embrace
I disappeared into his face
And woke uncomatose

And cured — the doctors did agree
First time that mere psychiatry
Had ever done the trick
To turn, in just some six years work
A simple sap into a jerk
And then to make it stick

Is medical advance indeed
Enough to make patients stampede
While rushing for the couch
The fact can never be obscured
Eventually I rose up cured
Of what? — I cannot vouch

In all my life I never heard
Of anything quite so absurd
Folly so neat and pure —
Why, when a racket's half this slick
You make sure customers stay sick
Last thing you want's a cure!

I'd tell the doctor all this stuff
Until you'd think he'd had enough
To make a medic rant
Just listen to your patients' dreaming
For thirty years — you'll wake up screaming
For a brain transplant!

Yet only once the learned doc
Broke down; he sighed, looked at the clock
Face almost seraphic
Took off his coat, mopped dry his brow
His misery confessed somehow:
"God what a lot of traffic!"

I patted him upon the back
And told him that his Pontiac
Looked real good parked out there
He brightened up and with relief
Pulled out his pad, tore off a leaf
And started to prepare

Himself for work, another day
He pointed, motioned, waved the way
For me to mount the couch
I'd climb aboard — like torture racks
Everywhere, to really relax
Confessing to some grouch

Is just about the only thing
That you can do, you've got to sing
Some kind of likely tune —
Upon psychiatry's dark bench
In dungeons, where the toenail wrench
Is used to make you croon

Even polite society
You'll find that even there you'll be
Practically pampered
If you tell what they want to know
Or want to hear, just let it flow
Totally unhampered

Say what you will, the truth, your dreams —
Reveal imaginary schemes —
Keep talking 'til you're blue —
Borrow your nearest neighbor's ear
Pretend there's something he must hear
Grab it and start to chew

It off in swift voracious bites —
Regale with images, delights
Don't wait for an answer —
Talk up a streak, jump down his throat
Denounce, insinuate, misquote
That Italian dancer...

You get the point; their attention's
Yours as long as what you mention
Borders on the taboo —
Ears will perk up, eager, twitching
Eyes — and you can see they're itching —
So, make their dreams come true

By never giving tongue a break
Like seismographs in an earthquake
Keep your needle waving
Go grab that fellow by the wrists
Write letters to psychiatrists!
Here's one I've been saving:

"To Mary Ann's psychiatrist
Who's got to be a specialist
In matters of the mind —
When probing through that tangled lace
Of nerves beneath her carapace
I caution you, be kind

Be gentle when you pick apart
Webs emanating from the heart
And strung throughout the flesh
Network of dreams, that tidal flow
Imprinted on the embryo
Especially what's fresh

The latest stuff, when you tread there
Please exercise abnormal care
Do not disturb the bloom
In that perfect... But doctor, dear
A problem of my own right here
I'm broken in my room

I've just raced home across the bridge
Remove my coat, start towards the fridge
And I spot the neighbor
Stuffing my wife up to the hilt —
My box of chocolate bon-bons on the quilt —
This calls for the saber

To clear the air of what might be
Misconstrued as un-neighborly
My wife, my bed, my brandy
A friendly visit during lunch
Is rectified with one swift punch —
But when they eat my candy…

I've kept a secret for some time —
Embarrassment, not lack of rhyme
Has made my mouth a seal
It is the con man's lucky break
That marks are too ashamed to wake
The world with their appeal

But when your pal, your trusted friend
Your partner who's supposed to send
You money that he owes
Calls up to say he's going to steal
Your share — of course he puts it real
Nicely — he even shows

The reason why he can't refuse
Some deal — the details would confuse
Me — it just looks so good —
So he's taking all the money
Shipping out to somewhere sunny —
I'd rather that some hood

Bitter, maddened from the ghetto
Press the point of his stiletto
Right up against my throat
Demand I give him everything
The watch, the credit cards, the ring
Even my overcoat

But when this "pal" — may his tubes rust —
Exercises his wanton lust
Not only on the girls
But on the cash he held. For shame
I cannot hesitate to name
This swine who stole my pearls

This vagrant cad who's done a few
Ultra-insidious deeds unto
Most everyone I know
Now that I check around a bit
I find the fellow's only fit
For making gardens grow

If you get my inner meaning —
I'll drop him in a vat where cleaning
Powder's manufactured
I'll push him off the window sill
Mix some concrete, but not until
Several limbs are fractured!

I must reveal his name to save
Other victims from this knave
Although I tried to wait
For a word, a sign, a gesture
Served no purpose but to test your
Patience, why hesitate

Why any longer should I feel
The slightest impulse to conceal?
I'll make of him fair game!
I'll tell the world about the guy
This slime, this filth is called... But, why
Immortalize his name?

YOU try to steer this ship through seas —
A hurricane proportioned breeze
Sweeping tons of water
Over the deck — the radar's lost
Nearly twenty degrees of frost
And the wife and daughter

Start complaining 'bout the rations
Also the accommodations
Are not quite up to par
Both radios have just gone dead
It looks like icebergs straight ahead
The nearest land's as far

As China, or the moon was when
It hung beyond the reach of men
We'll probably fall off
The ends of earth, the world above
Where Ocean meets the limits of...
I hear the engine cough

And sputter to a stop. Now all
The lights go out — a monster squall
Alright — we're going down
I've got to lower boats — and then:
"Are you ignoring me again?"
I thought at worst I'd drown

Or crack my head upon the deck
I've been through many a shipwreck —
Traveled most everywhere
I'm all composure, never addled
Until the wife with whom I'm saddled
Says: "I've nothing new to wear!"

Just when we're heading for the locker
Of Davy Jones — it's off my rocker
Is where she's driving me —
I wish I were already under
Fifty fathoms! — Although I wonder
If that would set me free

From this déjà vu I'm dreaming
Where the wife is either screaming
Or on the telephone
Chatting with some bosom buddy
Then the vision starts to muddy
Becoming overgrown

With random residue galore —
I know I've been through this before —
It's happening again!
Just like the words of that old song
I know that something's going wrong
But don't know Where or When

Then she'll relax a bit and let
Her body block the TV set
Which, of course, I'm viewing
Announce "I feel so bad today"
A confidence — then to the fray
"Just stop what you are doing

And take the kids out for at least
Several hours, you filthy beast"
And then she pulls her ace
"You'd better help me out, you ox
The children need bagels and lox
I've got to clean this place

So much to do before my hair
I can't stand you just sitting there!"
Her movements start to gain
Momentum, rise to fever pitch
The fury of an ancient itch
And now fresh waves of pain...

Smoking this stuff all night and day
Affects the memory they say
Even the chromosomes
Makes you stumble, falter, amble
Stammer, stutter, alter, ramble
So I just write the poems

And let the dummy say these things
While I sit back and pull the strings
And you guys watch the show
There's always someone in the crowd
Who speaks his inner thoughts out loud
Somebody says: "I know

He's real, just watch the way he moves
No dummy has so many grooves
Between such beady eyes!
It's just some wreck the poet found
Broken, he picked him off the ground
Just look how hard he tries

To pull it off — his stance, his clothes
That un-dummy like fleshy nose
Is giving him away!
A dummy has some kind of class
But this buffoon will never pass
I think he's going to say

Something in his defense to prove
He's a dummy — it would behoove
This chap to realize
That dummies are not made, but born
This creature looks like he was torn
Half out of his disguise!

How can he stand there unabashed
And pile before us mounds of mashed
Potatoes with gravy?
Does he expect us to swallow
Everything he says, to follow
This broken and wavy

Extravaganza, diatribe
Is it a speech? Come on, let's bribe
Someone to let us out —
This fellow's unprovoked harangue
Deserves an immediate meringue
To decorate his snout"

And then a pie somebody throws
Whipped cream on my mustachios —
It's better than a splint!
Sometimes the pie is lead or brick
Heaved by some struggling lunatic —
I'll leave you with this hint:

Find me reviewers, connoisseurs
Agents, critics, entrepreneurs
Producers of top shows
Movie moguls, T.V. magnates
Bring literary potentates
And impresarios!

Round them all up and fly them in
By helicopter, zeppelin
Whatever the pretext
In submarines, by motor yacht
Name your reward, I'll pay — if not
In this life, then the next.

canto four

WASHING DISHES

I'm excellent at making wishes
But when it comes to washing dishes
I'm nowhere to be found
My early ploy, when just a youth
Was showing them I was uncouth
By dropping on the ground

Some china dish, the finest piece
That I could find among the grease
Encrusted plates that filled
The sink where they expected me
To exercise some sorcery
And not get myself killed

Beneath the water, scalding hot
The charred and rusty cooking pot
The brittle, rotting slop
Deep down I'd probe, let fingers pass
Until they found some antique glass
Which I'd let loudly drop!

This worked for many years, in fact
I rarely need perform the act
For it had got around
And if the tale had not been heard
At washing time I'd drop the word
And thus avoid the mound

Of dirty dishes, filthy forks
Believe that babies come from storks
If you believe that I
Will ever wear the rubber glove
Sprinkle the liquid Ivory, Dove
I'll fight, I'll hide, I'll lie!

Do anything, I'll call the nurse
To free myself from this dread curse
I'll bite, I'll scream, I'll kick
It's gone beyond a parlor joke
(How many dishes have I broke?)
How many times played sick

When nothing else would work? When hosts
After I had devoured their roasts
Would lead me to the sink
Explain that they had heard the tale
How crystal, china, without fail
Would slip right through my pink

And really perfect finger tips
But now it's time to come to grips
And they were quite prepared
To see me through this washing chore
If I broke dishes on their floor
They said nobody cared

"We'd love to buy another set
Just try this apron on and get
Positioned here behind
The sink" — I thought I was the guest.
After dinner I like to rest
And I have to remind

Them of this fact, but they insist
Cajole and grab me by the wrist
Even a lunatic
Would see there's nothing else to do
I've got to carry this thing through
Watch out! I'm getting sick

Yes! I would actually do it
Compose myself, relax and spew it
Right there on the dishes
This usually was quite enough
To make mine hosts, however tough
Cater to my wishes

And when this story got abroad
Friends, relatives were really awed
And took especial care
Despite the most persistent itchin'
Never to mention the word "kitchen"
Whenever I was there

Now, in the Army there's a term
Used to describe the lowly worm
Who says that he is ill
Merely to avoid his duty
What a word — a sound of beauty
Yes, I can hear it still

Malingerer, malingering
It has a certain kind of ring!
Like lying in the shade
When there's a lot of work to do
Because your back is bothering you
Six months in the stockade

Will usually restore your tone
If you prefer to be alone
They have a little room
That's made for fellows four feet high
Where you can't stand or sit or lie
A kind of perfect tomb

So you can see, the way they deal
With fellows who sometime don't feel
Exactly up to par
Could cause an awful lot of tension
(And aches and pains that I won't mention)
To a nice teenage star

Who, the first time he drew K.P,
Confronted with a scenery
Out of some dream inferno
Went reeling back against the wall
Half blind, half mad. I could recall
Drinking a can of Sterno

With several hobos in the park
And feeling then the same grim dark
Shadow overwhelm me
I was in the devil's kitchen
(A place that certainly was rich in
The smell of mystery)

And there in sinks the size of pools
In stacks, in heaps, on chairs, on stools
Throughout the murky gloom
Someone had tracked down every plate
I had not washed since I was eight
And brought them to this room

And every single dirty knife
I had avoided all my life
Was staring from some pile
And spoons and cups and pots and pans
From youth were brought in moving vans
And talking all the while

The sergeant pointed out the slops
The soap, the lye, detergent, mops
He led me through a gap
Where ladles swinging on a hook
Formed an unpleasant sort of nook
And stopped at the grease trap

"Now after every dish is clean"
The sergeant said, while I turned green
"Before you take your ease
This trap must shine like polished ware
Or else you'll spend the night down there."
He forced me to my knees

So I could get a little taste
Of the aroma thick as paste
That wafted from the pit
In order to appreciate
The trap, he squeezed me to the grate
I figured this was it

And threw myself into a trance
(A ritual I learned in France
Which never yet has failed)
I blinked my eyes, produced a tic
Prepared myself to get quite sick
And soon my spirit sailed

Beyond this filthy horror show
I watched my body down below
      Writhing in a spasm
A twitching lump of flesh and bone
While I soared high above, alone
      Absolute — pure protoplasm

The soldiers watched with feelings mixed
The sergeant, perfectly transfixed
      Couldn't believe his eyes
Somehow, he grew solicitous
And started making quite a fuss
      And suddenly two guys

In white rush on the scene holding
Some object they start unfolding
      Which proves to be a stretcher
They toss my body in a heap
Then grabbing both the ends, they leap
      To the room of some lecher

Who's brandishing his stethoscope
And asking if there's any hope
      We might see each other:
"Later tonight, before the crowd
Makes my favorite bar too loud,
      Do you have a brother?"

And in a flash I realize
I'm on to something hot, a prize
If I can follow through
My soul returns to join the flesh
And while these subtle siblings mesh
Become just one, not two

It strikes me that I'm not so nervous
About the horrors of the service
I know I'll get out quick,
As long as there are fools to cater
To malingerers. The satyr
Doctor thinks I'm sick

And so do all the social workers
Psychiatrists and nurses — "shirkers
Don't throw up on the floor
They never go to such extremes
To prove they're ill — it only means
This chap is mad and more!"

Now when this story hit the vine
It grew like grapes, like tales divine
I never had to vomit
Just half a sound, or turn my back
Make a suggestion, not attack
And just like Halley's comet

Only occasionally performed
My bark was bluff, my warning stormed
So mighty is the tale
That once the word has got around
The act's not needed to astound
The images prevail

Before I knew, they let me go
Clean as a whistle, pure as snow
With only one small hitch
The General who had to sign
My papers on the dotted line
Came down with an itch

No one had actually seen
He realized, my guts careen
For quite a bit of time
And he'd be damned if he'd release
Some vagabond on a caprice
"Why, it would be a crime

To let this fish escape the hook!
By God, we'll do it by the book
Bring in the filthy rotter!"
I stood before his desk piled high
With papers, forms — I choked a cry
And did it on his blotter!

He tapped his silver riding crop
Upon the desk, a tiny drop
Of what I had let go
Adhered to it, around the tip
It quivered in his iron grip
He looked like he would throw

The thing or slash me in the face
Luckily, I had the good grace
To give him just a sample
I know that if I hadn't stopped,
He would have drawn his sword and lopped
My head off as an example

To several junior officers
Who turned themselves to perfect blurs
Getting out of the way
When I commenced my little show
His flashing sword would let them know
The order of the day

Stiff as a board, he slowly rose
His features frozen in the pose
Of one who has command
Surveyed his desk, inhaled the smell
He spots something on his lapel
And rubs it with his hand

Which only leaves a grimy spot
And on his hand a lumpy clot
Like something mixed with wine
His cool is blown, this cavalier
Who screams, roars: "Get him out of here
Remove this filthy swine!"

I'm whisked away like specks of dust
Are brushed from coats, with mild disgust
They take me from the place
And though I'm drummed out of the corps
And certified unfit for war
A smile's on my face

'Cause now I've got the right credential
For if I'm seen as a potential
Washer of unclean dishes
I merely have to let them know
Even the army let me go
Granted all my wishes

Rather than let me wash a plate
Off which some other soldier ate
I'm heading for the city
And civilized civilian life
I'll never wash a fork or knife
Again — I'm sitting pretty!

I buy a town and country car
Convertible, with built-in bar
Plenty under the hood
You know the kind, in brilliant red
White wall tires, a fold-out bed
Side panels made of wood

I live a life like other saps
Run round in circles, lots of naps
Make wonderful wishes...
And all the time, I never knew
The two of us were not yet through:
Me and dirty dishes!

So ten long years go by the board
I'm driving in a flatbed Ford
To North Carolina
To spend the summer in a camp
The Blue Ridge Mountains — and they're damp
As rice fields in China

Where mushrooms grow inside your trunk
And rhododendrons make you drunk
While hemlocks brush the sky
Some sixty kids from eights to twelves
Compose on cellos, follow elves
Through forests of July

A perfect paradise for me
I'm twenty-eight, write poetry
There's a new swimming pool
Which I'm to tend while saving lives
In such rare mediums, there thrives
Your common household fool!

Mostly, the dozen staff or so
Are teen-age kids, a college Joe
Except the following three:
The lady boss philanthropist
Her friend, a universalist
And then, of course, there's me

The three of us are long time pals
(Myself and these two older gals)
So I am quite surprised
When one evening before we dine
A bright young chap steps out of line
To see that I'm advised

That he and I are set to share
The kitchen chores that night "Look there
Your name is on the list!"
I stare at it in disbelief
But then I smile and with relief
I grab him by the wrist:

"So that's your idea of a joke."
"No, no," he says, and as he spoke
I saw that it was true
"So then, it must be a mistake
Go see if Vera is awake
So you can find out who

Really's supposed to help you out!
It's obvious, beyond a doubt
It's not my kind of task."
But Vera's nowhere to be found
My dinner starts to form a mound
A lump, my face a mask

I wait for someone to rush in
His cheeks magenta with chagrin
Announcing my reprieve
But no one does and by dessert
Humiliated, deeply hurt
Almost ready to heave

My living guts upon the floor
The table-cloths, the corridor
Because they dared presume
That I, in their most far-fetched wish
Would wash one single stinking dish
By now, the dining room

Is nothing more than vacant chairs
Half-empty plates, untouched éclairs
There's no one to be seen
Except the lad who's getting set
To do the kitchen minuet
Make everything come clean

And he's prepared to do it all
Because he doesn't dare to call
On me to lend a hand
With his young eyes, so bright, so clear
He sees me as a brigadier
A father in command

I'm in a spot, how can I leave
This boy, so innocent, naïve
To face the night alone?
And why get sick when no one's there?
I might as well try using prayer
To mend a broken bone

I just can't stand to see the kid
Take on alone this pyramid
Of garbage, fresh and canned
The stuff a camper-diner leaves!
To hell with it, I roll my sleeves
And give the kid a hand.

At last they've led me to the slaughter
My arms are deep in greasy water
This has to be the worst!
And now occurs the strangest thing
So eerie, so astonishing
I know I must be cursed

By Gods of whom I've never heard
I'm using steel wool on a curd
And pissed beyond belief
I plan revenge, I'm in a rage
(I'm steaming dishes in a cage)
And staggering with grief

I'm halfway through — the clean dish stack
Is filling up the drying rack
I feel a rush of blood
Shoot up my body to my head
It's warm and wet, I feel it spread
And now a raging flood

Of fresh, volcanic, raw emotion
Untapped and mighty as the ocean
Comes sweeping down on me
With every dish I wash and dry
The mood starts to intensify
I want to stop and pee

But my hands are going faster
I'm in the grip of some disaster
I wish I understood
Why, despite my lifelong training
Struggles, discipline, complaining
I suddenly feel good!

Wave after wave of bliss is rushing
Along my spine like wellsprings gushing
Streams of primal joy
That bathe in light, crown me with glory
Is this a True Confessions story?
I'm tossing like a toy

Caught in a whirlpool of delight
But now I'm putting up a fight
I think I see the cause
Why I'm floating in Nirvana
Omnipotent, complete, a Bwana
Against all natural laws!

Why this feeling keeps on lasting
Just like forty days of fasting
I'm higher than the sun
And on my face a stupid grin
When I'm up to my elbows in...
But wait, they're almost done

Only a few utensils left
(Which I now wash with movements deft)
Most everything is clean
To my disgust, I understand
Washing dishes makes me feel grand
Immaculate, serene

There's something in the act that's fun
Something about a job well done
To turn a filthy mess
Into a sparkling kitchen dream
So Brillo perfect, Ivory cream
A palpable success

Makes me feel wonderful, it's true
But sharpened slivers of bamboo
Are slicing through my mind
I hate the thought that I could feel
Magnificent, unique, unreal
Above all human kind

Just because I did the dishes
This kind of thought impoverishes
All my humanity
I'd rather be a silhouette
Irregular, depressed, than let
Such triviality

(A minor action, empty chore)
Determine when my heart should soar
And what about free will?
Some puny clean-up job can press
My button, make me effervesce
Make me an imbecile

Insane, delirious with joy
All set to dance at the Savoy
Or frolic in my bed
I don't mind feeling good at all
From drugs or sex or alcohol
Or standing on my head

Or Truth or Beauty, Nature, Art
These feelings all come from the heart
But when I just respond
To random pluckings on my string
When washing dishes makes me sing
I know I've gone beyond

The limits that a man must set...
Good God! I need a cigarette!
It's been so very long
Since I've laid hands upon a pack
I've had this monkey on my back
Whose grip was rather strong

I stayed away from smokes all year
Which made the monkey disappear
I thought that he was gone
But he was hiding deep inside
All doubled up and satisfied
Like a contented John

Dear lord, I want to feel the pull
Of drawing smoke, so rich, so full
Into my waiting throat
Caress the sweet unfiltered tip
With my impatient, eager lip
I think I shall devote

The rest of my remaining days
To lighting up, wrapped in a haze
Of blue tobacco smoke
In tiny rooms with curtains drawn
Unable to suppress a yawn
And puff until I croak

Well, almost twenty years have flown
Their course and I've long since outgrown
All youthful gibberish
I've concentrated on the deep
Dark mysteries of beauty sleep
And never touched a dish

Except to leisurely pick up
Some dainty item when I sup
Until six months ago
One night, while dabbling in ink
A voice told me to check the sink
Of my mountain chateau

I dropped my pen and started in
A prickly feeling on my skin
I saw a dirty plate
And several forks, a glass or two
Butter still out, running like glue
All left there by my mate

Or by the kids (perhaps the maid
In such a hurry to get paid
Just didn't notice them)
I poke around a little more
On the refrigerator door
Something that looks like phlegm

Is hardening to form a clot
Behind the chair I see a spot
And here's a touch of grease
Under the tablecloth that seems
So white and perfect that it gleams
There's dirt lining the crease

In fact, the more I look about
The more I think of dining out
The place is just a mess
The toaster, when you shake it hard
Drops crumbs — is that the smell of lard?
Look over here, why yes

This spatula is out of line
The coffee pot has lost its shine
This cap is not screwed tight
The ceiling? Dust. There is a stain
Upon the kitchen window pane
Maybe some dynamite

Would freshen up the atmosphere...
And suddenly, it's still not clear
I'm rolling up my sleeves
And scrubbing out this ring of grime
Beneath the drain removing slime
Because I know it leaves

An odor that I cannot bear—
I seem to smell it everywhere
I'd better mop the floor
And now, I'll use this stuff to bring
The tiles to a shimmering
A lustre. I adore

The early morning springtime smell
As liquid polish casts its spell
Upon the kitchen table
Deep in the fridge I wipe a drop
Of ketchup off the soda-pop
And luckily, I'm able

To find, where nobody would look
A fingerprint that I mistook
For a trick of the eye
By squeezing half my body in
The fridge and scraping off some skin
I wash and scratch and pry

Until the smudge is rubbed right off
Reacting to the cold, I cough
Then clean the fridge again
Because I'm sure, a deadly mist
Of germs the vegetables have kissed
I spot a specimen

Of some unusual insect
Dead in the lettuce, so I inspect
All of the food once more
I wash the salad greens by hand
And free the spinach leaves from sand
Before I close the door

And then, I dust and spray and mop
I brush and oil the counter top
I scour and scrub and scrape
I steel wool, polish, wash and dry
Powders, detergents, soaps apply
I'm getting things in shape!

I'm putting on my special glove
It's white on white — I reach above
The stove and I insert
A finger in that place so rank
(I've turned into a total crank),
There's not a speck of dirt!

So I relax, let down my hair
I'm feeling like a billionaire
The hero in a story
At home among his concubines
The sun is up, the kitchen shines
Like a laboratory

I trot across the street and see
Enveloped in the mystery
That married life affords
My neighbors — locked in deep embraces
A look of bliss upon their faces
It's better than drawn swords

I slip around to the back door
Tiptoe across the kitchen floor
Their house is a disgrace!
No matter, now my course is clear
I do the dishes — 'cause they're here
I clean my neighbor's place

And bring it to a perfect shine
While they play out the grand design
In bed, fulfilling wishes
I'm spinning on the karmic wheel
And manifesting all my zeal
By washing dirty dishes

I don't sleep much at night these days...
Has someone left the mayonnaise
Uncapped, outside the fridge?
I know that if I even think
Of dishes rotting in the sink
I start to hemorrhage

And bang my head against the wall
The only thing that helps at all
Is Brillo pads or soap
I have become a connoisseur
Of liquid wax and furniture
In fact, my horoscope

Suggests that if I play my cards
Correctly — and elude the guards
This is my lucky day
I'll say it proudly, unafraid:
I seek employment as a maid
I don't want any pay

To do a job you won't believe
The heights of cleanliness achieve
Make everything just right
I've cleaned up for ambassadors
Yes, I do windows, I do floors
Who'll take me home tonight?

canto five

MONEY

I find I definitely need
A lot of money to succeed
To keep affairs un-gummed
To make things flow without a hitch
To live the kind of life to which
I'd like to be accustomed

I started out with simple tricks
To milk my fellow lunatics
I'd place a dozen ads:
"Last chance to send your dollar to
Post office box Sixth Avenue"
And to discourage cads

And scoundrels, rotters, forgers, tramps
I'd write: "Please don't send checks or stamps"
To be perfectly frank
The money rolled in day and night
And I worked up an appetite
While jogging to the bank

And though this seemed a perfect way
To save up for a rainy day
And not even get bored
I soon found out some legal quirk
Made my rewarding, honest work
A classic case of fraud

Now, the master of the perfect scam
Finally wound up in a jam
Some fifty years ago
He found a way to make men smile
When lending money and all the while
Increasing his cash flow

I'm sure there's transference of thought
Somehow his grand idea was caught
Over the distant years
Up in the network of my mind
I too, would benefit mankind
Make profit without tears

I offered to give every week
Twenty percent — something unique
They stood in line all day
Waiting to hand me all their cash
And I'd return it in a flash
And every cent I'd pay

Including interest right on time
Upon demand, to the last dime
Till people got to know
A thousand dollars from some waiter
Would bring him twelve hundred one week later
So they would let it grow

And earn them interest while they slept.
Inspired by their trust I kept
A perfect set of books
If someone wanted money back
Why, John's deposit would pay off Jack
And all were safe from crooks

They made withdrawals from the bank
And brought me every single franc
We all were getting fatter
And even if there were a crash
And everyone demanded cash
It really didn't matter

For if I took in fifty grand
On Tuesday, money in my hand
And had to pay it back
Next week, including interest too
No matter when that debt came due
It would barely dent my stack

And every evening when I'd stop
And close my little money shop
I'd pause and I'd exalt
While watching strong-men take their pills
To lift those hundred dollar bills
And move them to my vault

Each day brought me new customers
My mistresses were wrapped in furs
I traveled much abroad
Until I woke up from this dream
I was engaged in a Ponzi scheme
Another case of fraud!

So I, who tried my very best
To share the wealth, help the distressed
To tighten up the slack
When I found out my ethic norm
Was judged officially poor form
I took a different tack

No longer making such a fine
Distinction of the legal line
The tightrope I was walking
I set up shop devoid of frills
My theme: "Good clients pay their bills
Without any squawking"

A dozen typists typed away
Two thousand bills were mailed each day
For fifty bucks or so
For service janitorial
For work on some memorial
A long, long time ago

One invoice more, a trifling sum
Another bill, some meager crumb
A hundred grand each day
Was regularly billed and sent
And without any argument
Forty percent would pay!

It is the capitalist fashion
To foreclose debts without compassion
So when they get a bill
They rarely take the time to check
If everything is up to spec
Before reaching in the till

Actually, some timid clerk
Who's doing all the dirty work
In Austin or Quebec
Is easily confused, misled
By our official letterhead
And just writes another check

It's easier to pay than ask
It is a monumental task
To put thoughts into words
That's why some passengers on planes
Who think they see the wings in flames
Pretend they're watching birds

They'd rather let the whole thing pass
Then prove themselves a total ass
It's still the same old song
What a choice, be roasted, skewered
Rather than to tell a steward
You think something's gone wrong

My bank accounts were growing huge
I swam in cash like Uncle Scrooge
I watched my world improve
Now only one thing spoiled my feast
Because of the nature of the beast
Each month I had to move

Some crank, out of the thousands who
Would pay their bill when it was due
Wasting company time
Would search the files, poke around
Until eventually he found
What he supposed a crime

And then he'd send out a report
Would try to drag me into court
Do everything, in short
To show himself a dreadful sport
To make my business abort
I'm sure you know the sort

So since I spent time on the road
And constantly changed my abode
I put into effect
A little plan I had devised
But never yet had finalized
To build my self-respect

I'd find a home that I could rent
More of a mansion than a tent
Comfortable and spacious
Lease it for just a month or so
In some big town like Tokyo
Where living's always gracious

I'd hire a girl to cook and clean
Her kid, as part of the routine
Would sing while he erected
A fairyland with little blocks
I'd put my name on the mailbox
(A name I'd pre-selected)

Soon all arrangements had been made
For this elaborate masquerade
And everything was ripe
You'd think I'd lived there all my life
My dog, my little kid, my wife
My slippers and my pipe

I'd advertise to rent the place
For half a year — this gorgeous space
This perfect paradise
To some upstanding gentlefolk
Who didn't drink and didn't smoke
At half the market price!

I'd see each one alone somewhere
The dining room, the kitchen stair
Even in the closet
Two hundred families arrived
And every one of them contrived
To give me a deposit

But most of them took me aside
And said they were so satisfied
"Excuse my being blunt
I see no reason to delay
With your permission, can we pay
The whole half-year in front?"

For several days I raked it in
I bought a brand new zeppelin
But the part that's really tough
When renting out someone's chateau
Is when to stop — it's hard to know
Just how much is enough

I handed out six hundred keys
To the front door, got guarantees
That everything was swell
To make so many people glad
Well, now, I'm off to Trinidad
As far as I can tell

I think with pleasure of the day
(Unfortunately, I'll be away)
When husbands and their domin
Eering wives arrive by twelves
To meet nice folk just like themselves
Who have so much in common

I just set up in some new town
I'm lounging in my dressing gown
And thinking that it's grand
This bonus of a thousand fold
Why rent? Three times this afternoon I sold
The house and all the land!

Now, money is a funny thing
It has a way of vanishing
Before your very eyes
It turns to food, to clothes, to smoke
This morning you were flush and now you're broke
No matter what its size

Your bank-roll is diminishing
It rolls away, a ball of string
That's always getting smaller
It disappears — the more you earn
The richer you become, the more you yearn
To be a social crawler

You must improve your way of life
Another mink coat for the wife
Take limos everywhere
A better college for the kid
You have become a financial invalid
While still a millionaire

So it turns out that you have pandered
Your very soul to raise the standard
Of living to a point
That's just beyond what you can make
And now you won't eat anything but cake
You hate the lousy joint

You live in, if you had some dough
You'd move into that smart chateau
And cater to your gout
Tonight you dine on roast gazelle
While several families do very well
On just what you throw out

You used to think ten thousand bucks
Was quite enough to live De Luxe
But now it's not the case
Ten thousand bucks! Your concubines
Drop that each month between imported wines
And lotions for the face

You dream you're floating in your yacht
In some imaginary spot
You've just received the news
That half the world is burning up
You and some billionaires sit down to sup
Onassis, Howard Hughes

The wine is excellent tonight
It stimulates the appetite
With brandy you all laugh
You have prepared for the event
The world is gone — almost fifty percent
But — you own the other half!

You and your friends have reached the place
Where there is nothing left to chase
You've taken all the plunder
Beyond what you can comprehend
So that, no matter what you ever spend
You're never going under

You dream, then wake in icy sweat
None of the world is yours as yet
But there're some bills to pay
After your scrambled eggs and ham
You'll have to start inventing some new scam
To get you through the day

Smoked sunglasses for an eclipse
Some lifetime bogus memberships
To an exclusive club
Perhaps you'll sell the Brooklyn Bridge
Convince an Eskimo he needs a fridge
Sell mermaids a hot tub

You married rich but soon went through
Your wife's entire revenue
In hardly any time
You sold her bonds, her deeds, her stocks
The jewels in her jewel box
Before you turned to crime

You sold her heirlooms in a pinch
Her wedding ring without a flinch
The sparkle in her teeth
You sold a hundred times again
You'd have her lift her skirts and then
You'd sell what's underneath!

Now, every man has got his price
Some want a lot to sacrifice
A mother or a dad
While some will sell a friend real cheap
For just a couple bucks, while he's asleep
Before he knows he's had

And some, who after selling all
The land, the house, the banquet hall
The stars out of the night
Their families, what's on the shelves
At last will sell their very selves
That's if the price is right

Now, every ten years here on earth
They celebrate the virgin birth
Of money and they choose
One man who soars above the rest
Who understands the ways of money best
And send him on a cruise

It's been a decade since the last
Official immemorial blast
With everyone aboard
So, the entire universe
Is wondering who'll win the purse
Receive the grand award

The fabled prize, mankind's acclaim
(That tarnished trophy cup of fame)
The tickertape downtown
The cruise, applause. The world waits stunned
To see who'll win the purple cummerbund
The Pearl Upon the Crown

On Wall Street shady financiers
Have staked their office staff's careers
On who'll win this event
While Moslems wager minarets
A well-known slum-lord-guru bets
Another tenement

They're betting thousand dollar bills
They're leaning out of window sills
And falling in the street
To place a few last minute bets
They're tumbling down past crowded luncheonettes
And landing on their feet

At home and off in foreign lands
They seek the man who understands
The nature of the beast
Who best of all can comprehend
Why God made money for the rich to spend
And he who has the least

Is usually the one who's picked
Some poor financial derelict
Who hasn't got a cent
Instead of bankers, oil sheiks
Or wealthy ocean-liner-owning Greeks
Or heads of government

Because the man who doesn't rate
A pot in which to urinate
Instead of on the floor
Who's penniless, deprived from birth
Is just the man who knows what money's worth
Not some inheritor

Who's filthy rich before he's born
Then drops a fortune to adorn
And pamper his new wife
Who pals around with kings at court
The wealthy man spends money just for sport
The poor man for his life

The principle is not elitist
God knows success is counted sweetest
By those who ne'er succeed
To comprehend a nectar (or
A dollar bill, a louis d'or)
Requires sorest need

And so, the field was narrowed down
By several judges of renown
To three pure saps who knew
Beyond all others, rich and poor
That no matter what discomfort you endure
You cannot take it with you

First, there's Slim Jim who's in New York
He's brushing roaches off his fork
Off his portfolios
The window's shut -—he'd rather steam
Than hear a hundred million natives scream
Above their radios

He lays his fork upon the plate
Pretending that the scraps he ate
Was some splendid dinner
And licks his lips like a gourmet
One hundred twenty pounds and every day
He grows a little thinner

The roaches fight for tiny scraps
The size of cities on world maps
They're bright-eyed and alert
Well-fed and sleek like millionaires
Perhaps they dine on grand buffets upstairs
Then drop down for dessert

His collar's frayed, his cuffs are worn
His one good pair of shoes is torn
The bottom of his boots
Is separated from the top
The shoes keep walking after his feet stop
His last pack of cheroots

Is crumpled, gone, and now he struts
Around the loft searching for butts
Something to ease the pain
Of several days without a meal
He almost slips on a banana peel
His leg starts in to drain

From an old wound that's really killin'
No money to buy penicillin
It feels like a grenade
Exploding pain without a pause
No money to buy dressings, to buy gauze
Not even a band-aid

Perhaps they'll have to amputate
Which won't help him to put on weight
Maybe some alcohol
Will elevate his mood — it's hard
When you're dealt the lowest possible card
To be above it all

If money isn't everything
How come it's so embarrassing
After a taxi ride
Or after dinner with a date
In some posh restaurant where you ate
The best they could provide

A touch embarrassing, I say
When afterwards you have to pay
The cabby or the waiter
The girl has started in to weep
She can't believe she's dated such a creep
A first-class second-rater

Your fingers fumble through your coat
Excuses tangle in your throat
The manager's discreet
He doesn't bother to suggest
The kitchen or immediate arrest
He just throws you in the street

Back home, the rent is overdue
Your clothes out in the avenue
The landlord isn't lenient
The rent's been due for half a year
You've spent your last buck on a glass of beer
It's very inconvenient

And over in Hawaii, Trace
(One more financial basket case)
Painting masterpieces
Is glad he isn't going back
To make another trip, he'd have to pack
No clothes in no valises

But in that tropic paradise
A very little will suffice
To get you through the days
Some cigarettes, a hunk of cheese
Bananas, coconuts, anemones
Grease burgers, Milky Ways

Also he finds he's more creative
Now that he's been going native
And learning how to live
Within the limits nature sets—
As long as there's a pack of cigarettes
There's nothing he won't forgive

He's selling works that are acclaimed
They're numbered, matted, signed and framed
With wire and a hook
Each one a perfect specimen
Five bucks apiece, then down to three for ten
If someone stops to look

But even if he works all day
Selling, no, giving them away
No matter what he earns
He'll never rise above the flaw
That marks him out a victim of the law
Of diminishing returns

And yet, although he'll never sock
Enough away to leave that rock
By some unnatural quirk
He's able to live very nice
In that quaint lava-covered paradise
With very little work

So, he'll put in two hours each week
Selling those gems, so rare, unique
With uncompromising zest
No matter what — unless that breeze
Holds just the slightest hint of rain or he's
A little bit depressed

This chap who's floating in the orb
Of debt, unable to absorb
The least financial shock
Uncushioned, broke, insolvent, flat
A monetary acrobat
Toppled, collapsed, in hock

Can you believe that with his mind
(The fellow's actually money-blind)
This simple, honest man
Composed an economic law
So perfect, so without a flaw
So cosmopolitan

So obvious, yet so obscure
Only a bona fide amateur
Could follow up the trail
And find the truth despite the odds
That principle inspired by the Gods
The non-sliding wage scale!

It came to him in crystal light
(And history will mark that night)
He woke up with a shout
He clearly saw the lean precision
The overwhelming brilliance of a vision
He saw beyond a doubt

That if every single human being
Knew that the state was guaranteeing
A thousand bucks a week
No matter what his occupation
From the leader of a nation
Down to a circus freak

Then everybody could relax
There'd be no words like income tax
Or how much do you make
Each man would get the same amount
With no deductions and with no discount
Or computerized mistake

And now economists all hail
The Trace Purcell non-sliding scale
With one majestic sweep
The plan unrolled itself at dawn
The vision struck, then passed — he gave a yawn
And fell right back to sleep

And out in old New Mexico
Young Tom twirls his mustachio
And thinks of the Marines
Where every day he had three meals
He's straining to remember how it feels
And wondering if it means

Despite how many stones you carve
All living artists have to starve
Perhaps another hitch
Since only after death, your art
Becomes so fashionable, so smart
And someone else gets rich

Perhaps it's just some cosmic joke
But when you're on the road and broke
Exhausted, starved and numb
From hitching rides all through the night
And waking up half-dead before first light
In some deserted slum

You almost have to laugh out loud
The sky is clear but there's one cloud
That's pouring down on you
A smart sedan goes roaring by
You have to laugh if you don't want to cry
There's nothing else to do

Ironic, when you think of all
The money spent on alcohol
The stacks of shining chips
You fed to the casino wheels
Like children tossing little fish to seals
The hundred dollar tips

You gave to everyone in sight
The bellhops, women of the night
You forced them on objectors
You'd stuff a C-note in the shirt
Of waiters just for coffee and dessert
Of newsboys, toll-collectors

To pay a bill, you'd flash a roll
Like something grown out of control
Immense. Out on the town
Chaps didn't drop a grand, you'd snub
You were a member of the Bwana's Club
The Pearl Upon the Crown

Remember when you bought the land
Where several cities used to stand
In the mountains of Peru
You paid the millions they were worth
Then flattened them into the earth
Because they blocked the view

And every time you met a girl
Who gave you just the slightest whirl
You'd buy her brand-new clothes
Give diamond rings at rendezvous
And now you're staring at your shoes
But you're looking at your toes

You used to have as many boots
As Sunset Strip has prostitutes
From every kind of skin
Iguana, serpent, ostrich, eel
So soft, there was no way that you could feel
What you were walking in

And now, if you had just one pair
To sell or hock or even wear
While standing in the rain
You'd count it as a stroke of luck
You'd trade those cobra boots for just one buck
To help you ease the pain

Another car comes racing by
Inside they all look warm and dry
They're slowing in the flood
At last, a ride — how grandiose
But no such luck, they're only coming close
To splatter you with mud...

Three fellows born out of their time
Between them, they might raise a dime
If each could float a loan
Like lovers who are never blessed
With the rewards of love, they know wealth best
As I have clearly shown

So, now's the time for you to make
Your choice, for God and money's sake
You don't need a machine
There is a simple way to vote
Write your selection on a little note
And enclose a flash of green

If everybody sent a buck
To their address, they'd wish you luck
And health and happiness
Just put one in the mail today
You'll never miss it, and by the way
Please send it out express

And there you have it, make your pick
If life's a game not worth the candlestick
You burn up in the playing
Take heart from Trace, from Tom, from Jim
And always use a first-class pseudonym
If you don't feel like paying.

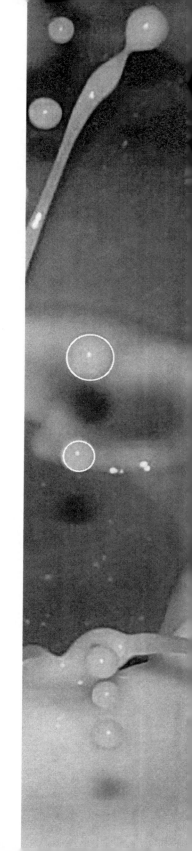

canto six

FRIENDSHIP

I know it's been at least a good ten years
Since I picked up The Pearl Upon The Crown
And scanning back in reverie appears
The best way to avoid a tumble down
For if I cracked that book again my ears
Would redden and my mirror show a clown
For who could look back with a calm reflective sigh
On his own early work and proudly say: "T'was I

Who writ this masterpiece, these perfect pages
I really knew what I was doing then
This stuff's immortal, why it never ages
And I'm still using the exact same pen
This work deserves to be there with the sages
No chance we'll ever see its like again"
Reviewing early work will leave a poet harassed
He'll not be proud, I think, more likely be embarrassed

And so right now I'm picking up my pen
And putting all distractions far away
I plan to try these cantos once again
Although I know the price I'll have to pay
Locked up for eternity in my den
The Muse, it seems, will always have her way
Once she engages you with her tantalizing
She's only satisfied with sheer fantasizing

But what's a decade more or less 'tween friends
For those who lived together through the worst
Who dove the ocean deep, contracted bends
Who recompressed together before they burst
Who bore the misery the desert sends:
Mirage, the blazing sun, exhaustion, thirst
And came up every time just roses, roses
Despite the flaws such intimacy exposes

For friendship is a very tricky thing
A bond so delicate and yet so stable
As fragile as a spider's silken string
As firm and fixed as a knotted cable
A friend will have no trouble pardoning
The worst offence, but will be quite unable
To bear indifference, the long crescendo
Of tone that crushes, the snide insinuendo

In order not to feel so all alone
So miserably single and bereft
To not be absolutely on one's own
Not be on the proverbial landing left
Not to be unutterably unknown
One needs to beg or buy, acquire by theft
At least one friend to help him navigate the stairs
And most of all to help outwit the billionaires

Friends can come in many different sizes
Fair weather friends, friends to the end are some
Appearing in a multitude of guises
The confidant, conspirator, the chum
The friend who constantly apologizes
Forever ad infinitedium
The buddy who is there when he is needed
Whose love's accepted, but his good advice not heeded

There is the good friend in the modern sense
Who'll rarely try your jugular to sever
Who offers you no threat of violence
And often keeps his finger off the lever
(Although he's bursting with omnipotence)
Of his spring knife, and who will hardly ever
(If you should chance to meet him in the lane)
Strike out in rage and slash at your face with his cane

Ah, friendship, the mere thought of which can bring
Relief from life's impossibilities
The summoned image of a friend can swing
My heart above it all on a trapeze
And from a wretched, broken underling
I soar beyond the distant Pyrenees
Complete in spirit, heart, in bone and marrow
Unleashed, in flight, on course, a targeted arrow

There is one friend among the rest who stands
Tall as a lily in a field that's rife
With countless weeds and thorns and shifting sands
Who for some decades now has shared my life
Her name is Linda with the lovely hands
She is my daughters' mother and my wife
To honor her in hopes she won't depart
For pain I've caused, I give her here my bleeding heart

The flowering cyclamen of fevered flame
I call it sickly-man so hot and red
Though just a houseplant beautiful and tame
With jungle foliage and crimson head
I brought it to regale today my dame
To sit in majesty close by her bed
Its awe-filled beauty hopefully will heal
The awful pain my lady's senses feel

All the friends of the very ill or dying
Cluster around him, come closer together
Old friends, not seen through years of Time's flying
About the pale invalid, light as a feather
Gather they near with eyes clear but hearts crying
From all over as if drawn on a tether
They circle about him like whales in the ocean
Protecting their young with the strength of devotion

I think of all the friends who have passed on
Into another place or other form
Friends who left recently or those long gone
Who slipped away alone or in a swarm
To other worlds or to oblivion
Whose clear remembered image keeps me warm
There's Tony Bellavia, Trace-Purcell
Count Albert Carlo, Peter Monk, Walter Chappell

Barry Bartels is gone and Tony Price
My Mom and Dad have made that final leap
From earth into the Halls of Paradise
All gone, but I still feel their spirits sweep
Me clean, their presence adds a pinch of spice
Sometimes they visit me when I'm asleep
Victor Maymudes and David Wheeler, all near
Pervasive essences, they drench my atmosphere

And very often make their wishes known
I'll feel a touch, a whisper in my ear
And suddenly I know I'm not alone
I call them with a thought and they appear
And it's as if we're talking on the phone
So real their voices are, so close and clear
As clear as living voices in my head
So far, thank God, I have more living friends than dead.

The telephone's not such a bad device
Although I really hate to hear it ring
And thru my blissful meditations slice
As shrill as a bird with a broken wing
Don't pick it up unless you want advice
Or gossip, slander, bad news, quarreling
Or care to learn about a relative's afflictions
It's hard to live without this worst of all addictions

The comfortable clasp of the receiver
That clings so lovingly to lip and ear
A caller never wants that touch to leave her
Nor the voice within the wire to disappear
Talk on thru meals, thru sleep, thru sex and fever
Despite hoarse throat, each day of every year
The telephone's not such a bad device, I swear
I talked with Bella yesterday and walk on air.

Now is that magic day that comes but once
A year when we've almost forgotten
That time can fly so fast, that life confronts
Us all, the blessed and the misbegotten
The rogue, the rosy rascal, sage and dunce
The fine and noble ones, the base and rotten
It's here before we know it's come again
And so I'm picking up my fountain pen

To wish you all the very best of luck
On a quarter century's completion
Without you running totally amuck
Like Shakespeare's jealous tormented Venetian
My lovely daughter I am wonderstruck
That you, like morning dew, God's secretion
Can wash my cares away with just the thought
Of the wonder that Lin and I have wrought.

I read that poem again the other day.
Many a time in the past forty years
Those words have leaped the page into my eyes
And always my thoughts travel the same way
I break into a smile and shed some tears
And maybe laugh a bit between the sighs
Remembering how you dreamed it would be
Three old white heads you and Barry and me

On a stretch of sand on a beach somewhere
The sun on our hands the salt on our skin
Watching the waves as they beat on the shore
And one of us sits in an old beach chair
And all of us watch as the waves come in
On a beach somewhere in the ocean's roar
Content, mellowed by all kinds of weather
Alone, just the three of us together

And this last reading now of Adam's Curse
Sent such a pang throughout my every nerve
To think that there is naught we can reverse
And naught but memories we can preserve
How a so indifferent universe
Will run right over us rather than swerve
Will leave us broken in its aftermath
To rise amazed and find ourselves still on the path.

Robo, I called. I left a ghost of thought
Upon your small machine that captures sound
To let you know that my whole being sought
To meet with you last week on your home ground
As for reply my message brought me naught
But my heart sings remembering what I found
When I stopped by late August last with Brent and saw
Magnificence of work that rocked me to the core

There were two paintings hanging in the hall
That I admired for a span of time
My nose against your workshop window wall
And many other things beyond sublime
I instantly desired to have them all
Before someone appeared like Guggenheim
Send me a catalogue tell me about the state
Your life, your mind, your heart is in, when can we meet?

I wondered why they called him Daddy Bill
Then Wendy told me that he had a score
Of children, grand, great grand, enough to fill
The house, twenty and half as many more
Enough to almost populate Brazil
And into each great draughts of love he'd pour
And by his strong example set the fashion
With tender kindness, patience and compassion

I heard he was an athlete his whole life
Played all the sports and worked out with the weights
For exercise ran circles round his wife
Around the house he'd race, thru doors and gates
His body and his mind sharp as a knife
Fine honed, balanced, a man who penetrates
Into the mysteries that life affords
To those who play upon her strings and sounding boards

Before the time of high technology
He spent his days in Service of The Park
Knew all there was to know about Hydrology
And in the National Guard he left his mark
He was a man who stepped out of mythology
And like a veritable Patriarch
Around the family fire each evening
He'd tell the ancient tales, play the guitar and sing

I heard two of those songs one summer's day
While great grand children splashed around the pool
Up on the hill with hosts Andrew and Gay
I heard Bill spin them from his golden spool
They made the sun and shadows dance and play
And thrilled us through to the last molecule
So, happy birthday, Bill, and keep on bringing
Your love and wisdom to us all and keep on singing.

When Cosimo di Medici and Joseph Schepps
Along with other Renaissance men of repute
Men who have reached the heights and plumbed the very depths
Whose lightest words are law, whose judgments absolute
When they stroll out on Tuesday morn they let their steps
Their velvet sandaled steps tread a familiar route
These demi-gods these jeweled ruffled charmers
Wend their way slowly to the market of the farmers

Across the golden cobbles of the castle keep
San Busco's mighty fortress greets astonished eyes
Its lofty spires lesser citadels out leap
And its innate magnificence electrifies
Straight thru the lawns and terraces our heroes sweep
While country folk step back amid admiring sighs
Displaying fruit, gourds and organic candies
For the pleasure of these lords and sultanic dandies

They circumambulate this early morning fair
Joined by some painters, two musicians and a poet
And taste the cakes and pastries country folk prepare
Throughout the long night's hours so that they now may show it
To lords and ladies who appreciate the rare
And who in fact would rather die than to forego it
They nibble, bite and munch on dainties thrust
Into their hands and mouths and chew with formal lust

While lutes are tuning up and painters making sketches
Our group of notables enjoys the changing color
An aisle of squash, a flaming row of ristras stretches
Around the stalls streaked gold by Autumn the Annuller
A nod and someone on the fringes runs and fetches
For Joe and Cosimo some coffee and a cruller
The poet pushes past a financier
And whispers these prophetic words into Joe's ear:

"Is not man strange? A thousand bucks a plate, Marquis
That's how successful fundraisers are always run
It gives the wolves a better chance of running free
Donations will not keep them from oblivion
So strange, despite my thousand bucks a word fixed fee
I left the price of my work up to you for fun
Advice seems to flow thru me like a sieve
If only I could follow the good advice I give."

I want to give thanks for the brand new laws
Concerning politics and other things
Especially the one exposing flaws
In ordinary men who would be kings
For now we'll see how fast a man withdraws
The hat he threw into the campaign ring
Now that the President's entire life will be
Broadcast on live twenty four hour a day TV

There'll be a special channel to be sure
So citizens can tune in round the clock
Confirm with their own eyes the Prez is pure
The house and senate solid as a rock
This job's no longer for the insecure
Now that the law says that they must unfrock
Tune in, you'll spot the Prez right off, no one can fake it
Look, the senators are all half, but the President's totally naked

Here's thanks to laws that make available
All public buildings to the homeless ones
That make men equal and all bailable
Those who have money and those who have none
That let no man be unassailable
Because of ancient name or modern gun
That lets us choose what we eat, drink and smoke
And choose the time and place when we decide to croak

And here's to that important social change
Made law, for which we all give heart felt thanks
Forbidding us from now on to arrange
Another meal from banquets down to franks
Without preparing on the kitchen range
Enough to feed one starved man from the ranks
For everyone of us who takes a seat
And feed them first before we all sit down to eat

Now Djordje and Betsy follow to the letter
All laws that are on books in our great land
And act as one, would rather wear the fetter
Than disobey the law's sacred command
And in this case they've done the law one better
I know that all of you will understand
If there's a little less for each of us to eat
Djordje and Betsy gave the turkey to the village down the street.

The Bears are leaving us for Hollywood
Awakened from their hibernating sleep
They stare out at the winter neighborhood
A snowy wonderland some six feet deep
And for a moment wonder if they should
Back in their downy feather beds all creep
But then they hear the distant strains of triumph call
For them to hurry to that coastal banquet hall

Where one long dining orgy of the senses
From morning 'til it's morning once again
Takes place so folks can maximize expenses
While entertaining all their fellow men
Who having lost their natural defenses
Rate every single movie as a ten
As long as there's a bag of buttered popcorn near
And the degree of violence extreme, severe

But then, that's what the public wants, they say
They've asked for dribble coming out the ears
It makes me sad sometimes that this array
Of talent, Hollywood, these sonneteers
Who could be bringing us a better day
By blazing trails to ever new frontiers
Will settle for another Golden Globe award
To prove that they're still celebrated and we're bored

But I'm not here to Hollywood indict
But to Milicevics sing farewell
As they go marching out sometime tonight
To take by storm the Golden Citadel
I know they're going off to lead the fight
For Art and Truth against the infidel
To set the stamp of beauty back upon the screen
And put some life into the Hollywood machine

To stand up like a team of grizzly bears
Who never will give way to anyone
But face to face in narrow thoroughfares
Will make the other fellow turn and run
Back down a studio of billionaires
Who'll lose that fight before it's half begun
The family Milicevic with flashing claws
Never from Truth and Beauty's fight withdraws

So keep the fire burning underneath the pot
Of coffee or of sake or of anything that's hot
And work away most of the day whether you feel like it or not
And try to have a good time in between
For all of us are keeping an eye upon the West
And all of us are wishing all of you the best
And all of us know where to go when we all need a rest
And some of that Milicevic cuisine.

I took a Yugoslavian freighter
From New York to Tangier some years ago
I saw a meteor create a crater
And must admit that it was quite a show
I watched police arrest a masturbator
For killing a potential embryo
Caught in this act illegal and improper
In his own garden spotted by a helicopter.

Maria Genitalia and Ricochet
Were always looking for in trance sting sex
No matter whether it be night, bidet
They turned their bodies into total Rex
And so they left the coast for Santa Fe
And found themselves in front of XZENTREKS
They needed to stock up on some devices
So they went in to check out all the prices

Now they had been to galleries galore
In every single country of the whirled
If X was on the signboard of a store
No time was wasted, instantly they hurled
Their bodies down the street and thru the door
In search of things that soothed, ached, slid, turned, twirled
They disregarded every least distraction
When they were on the road to satisfaction

They looked around and saw what we see here
And seemed at first a little disappointed
No videos, no whips, no panties sheer
No handcuffs to restrain the double-jointed
No special jars or herbal unguents near
With which to have their members well-anointed
They start to leave this strange familiar place
Get to the door and then their steps retrace

Magnificence of crystals catch their eyes
They stroke the gleaming shafts of fractured light
Marie lets one hand drift across Ric's thighs
And he rubs up against her body tight
Across the room heads turn hearing their sighs
Which quickly stimulate the appetite
And strike a note that deeply does arouse
All those who have come here to simply browse

In fact even the dimmest kind of nemish
Sees in those paintings hung along the hall
The artistry of masters of the Flemish
Dancing erotically down off the wall
Swinging those gorgeous buttocks without blemish
And whispering words of love in lilting drawl
Ric and Marie were right. Why make pretences?
There's not a thing here doesn't stir the senses

Into a turmoil of erotic thought
The mind and eye and ear are overcome
No wonder half the stuff's already bought
A kind of sensual delirium
Has rendered everybody's nerves as taut
As beaten skin on a pulsating drum
Even these ancient gems dug from Earth's core
Are throbbing like a sexual metaphor

Those Persian carpets glowing on the floor
Were made for sacred rituals of love
And several couples and now several more
Are playing in and out and push and shove
Until, my God, I swear, there is a score
Of lovers crying out to heaven above
As they the heights and depths of love explore
The magic carpets rise up from the floor

This is a pleasure dome, that's my testimony
Well, I suppose that it's to be expected
Those jeweled breasts, a lingam and a yoni
What kind of place has Andrew here erected
This music O so pleasurably drony
I am afraid we've all been Xzentrekted
By a Master of illusion and reality
Who's locked us in his palace of sensuality

Where time stands still, where just behind the screen
Those lovely ladies and mad gentlemen
His elfin helpers, gently intervene
And fill our glasses to the brim again
Ric and Marie depart, content, serene
A lovely night, a most unusual den
Is it Art or Sex or both? Who knows the answers?
Perhaps we'll find them in the movements of the dancers.

Now, don't you need a Poet on the payroll
To flash poetic license if you're stopped
To Cyrano-like feed lines for a hay roll
Immortalize moments that can't be topped
Who always can be counted on to stay droll
And Villon-like laugh while his head is lopped
Unmistakably, nothing could be saner
Than to keep a poet ready on retainer

The Poet lends a certain dashing air
A kind of grace, a subtle elegance
The right embellishment for an affair
Of state, of business, or of romance
The presence of a Poet shows you care
Enough not to leave anything to chance
Not to keep a Poet! What could be inaner
When one has a psychic, guru, valet, stylist, trainer?

Who else will turn an ode right on the spot?
To celebrate the closing of a deal
Compose a cancion red pepper hot
To accompany the triumph that you feel
Write epics for your mistress, horse, your yacht
And every day fresh wonders will reveal
Only the Poet has the perfect knack
To strip the Emperor's new clothes right off his back

Revivify the royal cloth and show
As if by magic what we've always known
That nothing is but thinking makes it so
That neither Emperor nor his new gown
In their magnificence can match the glow
That radiates from skin stretched over bone
Less uneasy is the head that wears the crown
When it's protected by the Poet or the Clown

The Patron needs the Poet there's no doubt
To swat the bee that's always in his bonnet
To turn confusing mists that swirl about
Into a clear and melismatic sonnet
Only the Poet merry and devout
Finds the right path and instantly gets on it
But then the Poet needs the Patron too
To stay alive so he can write this poem to you

So now you've got a Poet on the payroll
Who lies around all day and drinks your wine
Who hits on every woman for a hay roll
And scarcely ever writes a single line
A very slippery pure Santa Fe soul
Who vanishes and reappears to dine
Who's never there when you really need him
But, as I said, shows up when it's time to feed him.

I underwent a lost weekend experience
By answering an invitation to a lunch
Mine hosts prepared a vast array of succulence
Which ended up delivering a knockout punch
Gin fizzes all around they started to dispense
Served up with edamame beans on which to munch
The foamy splendor of the egg whites and the taste
Of lime and heavy cream all worries soon erased

I drank at least a half a dozen by my count
And felt my being gently float without restraint
While everybody else poured down twice that amount
And more, without the slightest hint of a complaint
I sipped again from that free flowing gin fizz fount
And felt the glow of warmth you feel before you faint
Soon all the bubbles in my blood and brain exploded
I was perfectly balanced and perfectly loaded

Then came a couple trays with silver dollar size
Buckwheat pancakes with radish sprouts and salmon smoked
Our host had flown to Chile to aromatize
That fish he caught there and he personally stoked
The smoke house fire and now presented us this prize
Whose delicate pink flesh immediately provoked
The one response, we held our glasses up, and then
Toasted our hosts, who filled them to the brim again

It's a wise host who knows far better than his guest
The time has come to switch from gin to beer and wine
And though this move made us a little bit distressed
Because we doubted anything could be as fine
We soon forgot and drank the red and white with zest
As we were served a course grown on a different vine
Squash blossoms stuffed with wild salmon mousse then rolled in
Eggs and flour, sautéed not golden brown, but golden

Along with this there came a lively dip of cream
With bits of Kalamata olives sprinkled round
These tasty toasted blossoms bloomed more than supreme
The pleasures of those tastes still on my tongue abound
I caught myself slipping into a lovely dream
Where every little thing in alcohol was drowned
Our hosts bade us arise to take a walk across
The grounds: arroyos, juniper, cacti and moss

When we returned about a half an hour later
Refreshed and ready to resume our sumptuous feeding
Our hosts who were quite determined they would cater
To every single whim went on with the proceeding
Preparing us a soup to satisfy a satyr
Which after refills sent us instantly stampeding
I think its origin was somewhere in the Congo
I had a beer and learned they called it Bongo-Bongo

I must describe this soup that was so very rich
But first before continuing I have to note
I knew exactly what the hour was 'pon which
We first arrived, when I began to nicely float
It was just two, and now I saw that it was six
The odds this feast would ever end were quite remote
We drank with spoons, we sipped right from the cup like birds
And after seconds of this soup we called for thirds

It was concocted of these elements I'll name
Some sautéed leeks, steamed spinach, very young and green
Two pounds of oysters cooked on just a tiny flame
All thrown into the blender, whipped by the machine
To a puree, a touch of curry powder, wild yet tame
We finished off the soup, and lo, time for caffeine
A few rounds of "Post Alley Speedball Queens" 'twas called
Double expresso bourbons in case your engine's stalled

Then we volatilized a bit, some wine, some beer
The hosts prepared a pasta radiatore
Little radiators, the next course to appear
That matched the morels in the sauce, which gave it glory
We all agreed this dish was something to revere
Just like that time in... But that's another story
I walked outside alone to make a water-mark
The stars were shining bright, it was completely dark

I glided back inside in time to see the change
Of platters, dishes, plates and under plates. The glasses
Were being filled afresh with wines both rich and strange
I heard the mellow tone of talk 'tween lads and lasses
The pleasant murmur of musical depth and range
Lost in the afterglow of dining that surpasses
When what should greet our eyes but a simple salad
Wearing garlic dressing, worthy of a ballad

Well, that's the end. There's nothing more to say except
That as we struggled to our feet to start for home
A raspberry sorbet with strawberry slices stepped
On to the table like an Emperor on his throne
Double expressos, creamed, with bourbon too. We wept
And while we ate and drank eight happy hours had flown
I'm used to dining country style, you know, hog in trough
But after this all I can say is: Stanley, Rose, hats off!

"I would have been here sooner but my car
Exploded when I put the thing in first
And when I realized how very far
I had to walk an overwhelming thirst
Forced me to run into the nearest bar
Where I imbibed until my bladder burst
And then I tried my best to call you on the phone
Which didn't work because there was no dial tone

I hailed a taxicab to rush me here
I didn't want to make you have to wait
But something noxious in the atmosphere
Made my poor heart begin to palpitate
I thought I better have another beer..."
"Excuses, friend, I cannot tolerate
How many times must I tell you, it's just good sense
Self justification is worse than the offense."

I wish to celebrate that summer day
Exactly fifty years ago from now
When Charles and Danny promised they would play
At house, and swore a ceremonial vow
I was not there so every thing I say
I heard from Carola, to whom I bow
She told me all the details of that wondrous morn
Although my calculations show her not yet born

They said there was no way that it could work
To marry someone she met on a boat
A poet, thin, divorced, mad as a Turk
Outrageous, proud, a stick in a tattered coat
And though his duty he would never shirk
He stood out like a sore thumb or sour note
Among the perfect rows of proper Quakers
Like a mistake made by incompetent match makers

And then as if that weren't quite enough
Arrives in a police car Charlie's aunt
A frumpy, blowsy whirl of powdered fluff
As bouncy as a fresh blown debutante
Producing from her magic powder puff
While saying to an offered drink: "I can't"
A box bought at a fire sale, which effervesces
Ten identical pink half-singed baby dresses

When no religioso could be found
They thought the wedding was completely sunk
But after searching all the hills around
They dragged a preacher from his backwoods bunk
And though for preaching he was not renowned
He was revered as an outstanding drunk
A German Jew, the best man, profound and hearty
Rounded out the groom's side of the wedding party

Then in the warmth of summer's opulence
Wrapped in the fragrance of a flower's caress
Out of the house, along the picket fence
White, white as the bride, white as her wedding dress
To the garden in her magnificence
Steps Danny daintily and blemishless
Before, around her spreads a heart-rending perfume
As buds, waiting for this moment, burst into bloom

And trailing after like a wedding train
A dozen ducklings scurry on the grass
They follow Danny down that lover's lane
Which other earthly joys cannot surpass
Not even joy of bubbling champagne
Nor travels through the famous looking-glass
Despite a world of nay sayers who disparage
Can match the joy of lovers love locked in marriage.

I wrote somewhere how friends you rarely see
May well be those you feel the closest to
No need for physical proximity
Why long to have someone always in view?
It's quite enough to know right here is me
And elsewhere in this universe there's you
Invisibly accompanying each other
Apart, but inextricably one another

I said I wrote these lines and this is true
I jotted down on paper with my pen
Those words about how very close to you
Some friends can be, unseen since who knows when
But I would need ten years to rummage through
The monumental shambles of my den
To find those words, those lines, that yellowed page
That tattered, torn and crumbling sheet, faded with age

It's not a pretty sight that greets the eye
When first confronted with a tower of notes
Great stacks of books and pads heaped up so high
A skyscraper of words that sinks and floats
Half-buried manuscripts that groan and cry
A feast for termites, bookworms, Billy goats
To search this pile of such extreme proportions
You must perform octopodiacal contortions

But, better yet, let's just forget about it
I wrote those words, already told you so
Once is enough, there is no need to shout it
Or to explain how mold and mushrooms grow
On aging rags of paper, no, I doubt it
Worth the candle used to light the studio
I only mention all this trivia to stall
Because I think I hear my Muse about to call

And when she beckons I stand up, salute
And pay attention to her every word
For her pronouncements are most absolute
And to ignore them would be as absurd
As pulling out a flower by the root
Or strangling the loveliest song-bird
For nothing in this world can so seduce
As when the Goddess wraps me in her silken noose

And whispers in my ear a healthy measure
Of words and song to pass all men's believing
It fills my vessel up with such sweet pleasure
To listen to her endless interweaving
And then to top it off she grants the leisure
To work new wonders of my own conceiving
And I, her glory praise with a Te Deum
My Muse, the Queen, whose home's the only real museum

And She's reminded me there is a link
Between close friends you hardly ever see
And those who've danced away beyond the brink
Somewhere between despair and ecstasy
All kinds of friends, it really makes you think
Stalwart, demure, some cloaked in modesty
Outrageous, strong, unclassifiable
And everyone unique, that's undeniable

The stance, the attitude, the way you deal
With friends who died and those who're far away
Is much the same, you can't enjoy a meal
An after dinner drink with them, a play
Whether they're here or spinning on the cosmic wheel
In Timbuktu or on the Milky Way
Whether at heaven's gate, a palace or some dive
Good friends are harbored in the heart, dead or alive

And harbored in the heart they're always there
In that special spot you've allocated
For friends, both gone and far away to share
Their essences, distilled and concentrated
You're less uneasy in your easy chair
Knowing your friends, both here and transmigrated
Are gathered in your heart and quite at home
Much too relaxed and comfortable to ever roam

The difference, then, between the dead and dying
(For all of us are dying right from birth)
Between the quick and those who now are lying
In urns before they're scattered on the earth
Or graves before the soul goes butterflying
From sullen tombs into a world of mirth
The difference, then, between the two is very small
Perhaps, like death and sleep, not very different at all

Mankind feels sad after the little death
Referring to the swift orgasmic gush
And in the time of Queen Elizabeth
The verb to die meant the climactic rush
Which lasts as long as you can hold your breath
But closer still to the eternal hush
There is a little death for which we do not weep
It is the full third of our lives that's spent in sleep

The friend, the lover and the boon companion
Whose fellowship and trust is manifest
Whose strength and enterprise are like the banyan
That turns its shoots to roots and stands the test
Of time, whose spirit from the deepest canyon
Soars up above to reach the highest crest
Such friends, when they're "at one within their inmost hearts"
(As a short poem attributed to Confucius starts)

"Shatter even the strength of iron or of bronze
And when they understand each other in their inmost heart"
(The poet of the long ago by-gones
Continues in his fashion to impart)
"Their words" (they can be beautiful as swans
When linked together by this master of the art)
"Their words are sweet and strong like the fragrance of orchids."
Fraught with significance like stars and pyramids

I had a friend when I was nine or ten
So long ago my memory grows dim
We were inseparable; his name was Ben
Or Gene. One day upon a crazy whim
He took my stick and wouldn't give it back again
And after that I never spoke to him
I thought it was unjust; neither of us would budge
And I spent twenty years or more nursing that grudge

So clasp a good friend to you, hold him tight
Strive to avoid discordant notes that jangle
Let hearts and souls in fellowship unite
And steadfastness the knotted threads untangle
Be equal friends, not host and parasite
Be always close, but not close enough to strangle
Defend each others honor to the end
And trust him with your life, but not your wife, my friend

If all of this seems very complicated
You're not the only person in the boat
I just relate the thoughts my Muse dictated
Verbatim, word for word, I don't misquote
And if you think, somehow I've overstated
And my images are blurry and remote
Don't puncture my side of the boat, thinking me daft
Because, you know, we're all here in the same rubber raft

The end of last millennium was marked:
Not able to eat, sleep, shit, smoke or fuck
As if somebody accidentally parked
His brand new fully loaded pick up truck
Upon my throat and belly and remarked
On noticing me underneath: Good luck!
So random, casual was the hit I took
A thrown coat, sliding down the wall, that missed the hook

But now I'm slowly pulling out of it
Some of those holy pleasures have returned
Here I am out making a night of it
With friends whose friendship has most brightly burned
Telling the last one thousand years to shove it
Although I know there's something we have learned
That there's an immutable link, a bond
Connecting everything before, right now, beyond

And all of us from stardust were created
And everyone to stardust will return
Within five billion years our sun is fated
It's customary movements to adjourn
Leaving everything incinerated
The earth a final funerary urn
So that our dust and ashes may be spilled
In space, new galaxies and life forms to rebuild

So what's a thousand years or so 'tween friends
Each hundred years a century will come
Time's just a way to count; it never ends
Ten centuries make a millennium
How fast or slow it goes, that all depends
A nanosecond is too long for some
A million years flies by in just a blink
For distant stars burning on the galactic brink

And cuddled cozy round this glowing fire
We celebrate the passing of the years
If they, about our little lives inquire
We'll say they're sprinkled with some laughter and some tears
We're ready for whatever might transpire
Knowing the spirit always reappears
And even living flesh and blood and bone
One day upon the Master Potter's wheel
Into new golden vessels will be thrown.

canto seven

EVOLUTION

Now has that deep and gorgeous dreamlike night
At last arrived, and on our souls descends
A cloak of mystery that filters light
And muted tones of dawn and evening blends
Into an ambience so darkly bright
Our vision of the universe extends
Beyond the stars into the land of never
And we can only hope this night will last forever

I want no long day's journey into night
Enough of day, I will build a palace
Out of a single stone, a meteorite
Beneath the grand aurora borealis
And spend my time in darkness and delight
Sipping hot wine out of a frozen chalice
And when I see the midnight sun unroll
I'll pack my bag and travel to the southern pole

To always be in darkness, in the cool
Folds of the blanket of black night's relief
Free from the stark and glaring ridicule
The blazing sun beams down, time-burning thief
Tucked out of sight in some well shaded pool
A shadow pocket of this star swept reef
Give me a cave, a hole; tuck me away
Where I won't have to watch daylight's dreadful display

Sometimes I have a most insistent urge
To be completely wrapped in a cocoon
Tossed into empty space beyond the verge
Protected from the fiery sun of noon
To float in peace and never to emerge
Until I reach the dark side of the moon
Escape from dreams of steaming hot equators
And dwell alone among the chill and starlit craters

Cool is comfortable and hot is heavy
These are the facts; it's just scientific
I'd rather be surrounded by a bevy
Of icebergs, glaciers, things all frigorific
Than sweating here inside my beat up Chevy
Stuck in traffic in the South Pacific
It's much too bloody hot on islands tropical
As hot as Hell, and just as misanthropical

There is a reason for most everything
If you can find the kernel in the chaff
A reason why the bee has got a sting
And for the ten foot neck on the giraffe
A reason why the world's unraveling
And why we watch it fall apart and laugh
Why Heaven's cool and placid as a lake
And Hell and tropic islands hot enough to bake

Now I don't want to be misunderstood
Heat is okay, to fry your morning bacon
Nothing is absolutely bad or good
Cold water on the face helps you awaken
Bright day is night's reverse, in all likelihood
Unless, of course, I'm terribly mistaken
And I can tolerate both day and night
And ten below as well as ninety Fahrenheit

But what I most enjoy is where they meet
Like black and white within the yin yang sign
First light of dawn before the day's complete
The sky at twilight streaked incarnadine
To take, after the hot spring's soothing heat
An icy plunge to loosen up the spine
To reunite extremes of things and places
For opposites are but the one coin with two faces

Yes, opposites are really counterparts
You can't have one without having the other
Just take the case of lovers and sweethearts
Or study why, when you can't breathe, you smother
But this example ends before it starts
It's meaningless -- I'll have to find another
Some other way to tell you what I mean
Good God, I'm lost; let's hope my Muse will intervene

"Hail, Muse etcetera" is how Byron begins
One of the cantos in his great Don Juan
A mock-heroic poem that surely wins
And in its time considered quite a new one
Note in pronunciation how he spins
Rhyming the hero's name with words like true one
Replacing the conventional Don Juan
That rhymes with words like flan and Parthenon

So, while I'm waiting for my Muse to fly
In circles round my empty scatterbrain
And in her usual fashion to supply
Those things that by myself I can't attain
Like some sort of a decent alibi
For rambling on and getting lost again
Let me quote a Byron stanza, not too shoddy
Which, the spirit of the mock-heroic, doth embody

"I would to Heaven that I were so much clay
As I am blood, bone, marrow, passion, feeling
Because at least the past were passed away
And for the future—but I write this reeling
Having got drunk exceedingly today
So that I seem to stand upon the ceiling
I say the future is a serious matter
And so, for God's sake, hock and soda water!"

"Now I have seen the future and it works"
These words from some extremely clever fellow
Not just one of your ordinary jerks
Who greets you with these sounds instead of "hello"
But still, there's something sinister that lurks
That doesn't make you comfortable and mellow
The worst things can work well like slavery and war
Like Orwell's future vision of nineteen eighty four

The future is a very serious matter
Which doesn't mean that we can't laugh about it
Why, every day it's served up on a platter
And we can hardly carry on without it
Just treat it properly or it will splatter
Egg on your face; can you wipe it off? I doubt it
Think that the past is dark, the present barely known?
Just wait until you're hurled into the future zone

"You don't have any future as an actor"
How often have you heard that same old song?
"Don't give your day job up, driving a tractor
Don't call us, we'll call you in the future, so long"
These lines from the purported benefactor
Trying to make you feel that you belong
Such folk think they can look into your future
Then cut you open with their vision, like a butcher

Many profess to see beyond today
Foretell the coming of unknown events
Look at the lines that mark your palm and say:
"You're headed for a life of opulence
A lover comes to whisk you far away
A dark and handsome stranger, rich, intense
Who wears upon his chest a jeweled medallion
And takes you, at full gallop, on his golden stallion"

There're those who, in the movements of the stars
Spend their whole lives in ceaseless pondering
Who know about all the particulars
Of the small fortune you are squandering
Who'll show conjunctions of Venus and Mars
And other planets in their wandering
About the heavens above. They take one look
At the celestial motions and read them like a book

Or you can learn the future from the bumps
That dot your skull from a phrenologist
If you prefer the fire's flaming jumps
Go find yourself a good pyrologist
If you don't mind taking your share of lumps
A chat with your friendly theologist
Will help you see beyond this life on earth
Into the future and evaluate its worth

There were, in ancient days, those cryptic lines
Sung by the priestess of the oracle
That told the future, pointed out the signs
The paths to follow, back in times historical
The potency of sacred temple wines
Revealed the world in visions metaphorical
The cloudy meaning of the revelation
Varied according to each one's interpretation

The patterns tea leaves make in cups of tea
The ramblings of a dying man, his groans
The ravings of the mad in ecstasy
The shape and form of polished river stones
The thousand different types of augury
Practiced by man in caves, in huts, on thrones
All divinations strange and curious
Believed by seekers to be true, not spurious

The aura glowing round each human being
Can easily be read by those who know
The psychic, whose strange power of foreseeing
Is waiting for you on her TV show
The fortune teller, your future guaranteeing
Sees in the crystal ball or the Tarot
What life holds in store, and for a gratuity
Will tell you all, through mists of ambiguity

To look into the future, try Miss Nancy
She knows exactly what will happen when
An adept of the art of necromancy
I'll show you how to find her charming den
Or if you think this might be a bit chancy
I have a friend who uses, now and then
Some jungle herbs she whips into a potion
One drink and you will see the future in slow motion

There is an eye that's looking toward the future
We come in contact with it every day
While waiting for tomorrow to occur
It calmly stares ahead and points the way
And though we often see it as a blur
It keeps an eye on us each time we pay
Its steady gaze as piercing as a drill
Atop the pyramid on every dollar bill

Egyptians used the pyramids as tombs
(Whether they built or found them there is moot)
The royal bodies placed in little rooms
That launched them off into the absolute
Bedecked in most magnificent costumes
With all their goods accompanying them en route
The mummies in the mummy cloth were wound
Projected to the stars above, yes, future bound

They lived their lives with a vitality
That like a circle never seems to end
Refused to dwell upon finality
A word they could not even comprehend
They sought a kind of immortality
Which meant, into the future they'd ascend
Wearing the sphinx's inscrutable smile
At home, as if they still were lounging on the Nile

The pyramid, designed for star ascension
A late and famous unknown thinker says
Is a perfect model of the fifth dimension
He learned some secrets in mysterious Fez
His spirit spins in heavenly suspension
While his ashes ride the salt sea of Cortez
His sides so split with laughing, I know he'll need a suture
As he goes madly dancing up and down the future

We thought the future was a rosy dream
Before the bomb blew up that pleasant myth
Life was a piece of cake, peaches and cream
Beneath the chestnut tree the village smith
Beat out the cheerful note of our regime
We were not ready to believe that with
The stunning power of a single blast
We could eradicate the present and the past

And drop upon this happy stage a pall
A somber curtain that came tumbling down
Over the future, everything and all
And changed that rosy dream into a frown
We felt an overwhelming darkness fall
That blindly crushed The Pearl Upon The Crown
And sent us scurrying into our holes
And left the future with no one at the controls

And though each day we're dropping off like flies
Nothing disturbs the glowing inner jewel
The death of flesh lets spirit etherize
Our essences survive, not the residual
This is the way; there is no otherwise
There's only short term for the individual
Whose body turns to bones and fossil feces
The long term future's for the race and for the species

This vehicle, this crate, this earthly form
Composed of flesh and bone, of nail and tooth
These creatures who upon this planet swarm
Whose bodies can do anything in youth
One day grow old, their blood no longer warm
They fall and rot, decay; to tell the truth
They hope to see the future through their progeny
Unless they've been practitioners of misogyny

A man is not immortal, but the race
Can make a bid for immortality
Evolving for itself a brand new case
To bring the soul and its new mentality
Into the unknown rigors of deep space
At last replacing animality
Which, after all, is just the current dress
With a better vessel, that's perfect, blemishless

The dinosaur did well, the horseshoe crab
The roach is nearly indestructible
The swordfish grew a sword and learned to stab
Extinction is not ineluctable
Mankind will go to space and build a lab
Being a creature who's instructible
Evolve and change, adapt and grow with no commotion
Sharks lived three hundred million years under the ocean

And though we all are born to reproduce
And through our children live in future time
That inner glowing jewel that flows profuse
The spirit, force, that essence so sublime
Yes, the immortal soul turns on its juice
It rises up above the body's pantomime
And finds another form for its next habitation
But only if you believe in multiple incarnation

If every part of universal soul
Which now resides among the population
Six billion, covering the earth from pole to pole
Lived up to its immortal reputation
Then we could shed our husks, each piece becoming whole
No longer chained by differentiation
And every portion rising bodiless
Like shimmering drops of mercury, would coalesce

And we would all be one, and live forever
Immortal parts become immortal soul complete
And with this monumental-like endeavor
We'd walk upon the sunny side of heaven's street
Rejoicing in the thought that we will never
Again dwell on the body's death, the winding sheet—
To want and seek the whole, is love—ambrosia
As Socrates has pointed out in the Symposia

Be one and live forever— Our dogs and cats
If they could prove they had a soul too
Could also leave their bodily habitats
Along with all the animals, the gnu
All forms on earth and sky and sea, trees, gnats
All sentient beings would pass their spirit into
The universal soul and drop their outer wraps
Of mortal clay to fall, unneeded back to earth, collapse

For bodies are a big pain in the ass
Except for the occasional caress
They're always sick or breaking down, alas
And needing rest and quiet to convalesce
If only they were made of steel or brass —
Imagine carrying the mail Pony Express
Back in the days when nothing else was faster
Nor many a stretch of open country vaster

A rider rode for ten or twenty miles
Pushing his horse to gallop at top speed
Through canyons, rivers, steep ravines, defiles
Most mercilessly urging on his steed
Ignoring all, along this trail of trials
The dust and heat in his headlong stampede
Through hills of cactus, tumbleweed and purple sage
Until he finds himself completing the first stage

Jumps off the horse, runs to the hitching post
Without so much as stopping for a breath
Leaps on the fresh and saddled horse that stands foremost
(His former mount is gasping half to death)
And, mail in hand, he charges toward the coast
The first stage done; and by the twentieth
He is a little tired, but he's really feeling swell
While twenty horses down the trail are beat to hell

This man upon the horse, this rider, is the soul
Who's always riding onward day and night
Who fills the empty body like milk poured in a bowl
And when the man and horse, the soul and body unite
This combination prances toward its goal
And fills the empty vessel with delight
He uses many horses and leaves them when he's done
The horses pale, exhausted; the rider moving on

What if we traveled on the road not taken
Instead of strolling down the one we did?
It might lead us to fairylands forsaken
And send our lives into an endless skid
Or maybe we would instantly awaken
And learn the secrets of the pyramid
At every crossroad futures various
Are waiting for us, strange and multifarious

If you could look into the great unknown
If you possessed that capability
To know which road will lead you to the throne
And which meanders to futility
If you could have the future clearly shown
Things would work out, in all probability
If only you could get a little whiff
Of what's to come, you could relax— but only if

O, if we had a pocket oracle
That we could bring with us where'er we go
Who plainly spoke, not waxing allegorical
And told us everything we want to know
We'd not be up the creek without a coracle
Caught in the blues of that mood indigo
If only we could have some solid facts
A map of future roads showing the cul-de sacs

If only we could perfectly forecast
The future, find some prophetess who's famous
Some sibyl, seer, witch who's unsurpassed
Some augurer who's not an ignoramus
Who would translate the future book, a metaphrast
So we could understand it, a Nostradamus
Who always is available to tell
The future, to Monsieur and Mademoiselle

Now once upon a time when nothing was
Or everything was chaos — both the same
The far off sound of a pervasive buzz
Turned all that was or wasn't into flame
As, after a big bang it always does
And into being, universes came
All part and parcel when you're dealing with
The many variations of the creation myth

And on our planet circling a star
Where life forms of all kind are surely thriving
We notice that these processes still are
At work, great forces at the core contriving
To pierce the ocean's surface like a scimitar
And from the deep sea floor are thrusting, driving
New islands up, with energy terrific
To rise above the waters of the great Pacific

And these new lands were barren, like the earth
In early years, just fire, rock and ocean
When nothing lived within the wide world's girth
Until a spark, a flame, some magic potion
Ignited that sweet miracle of birth
And single cells, inspired with locomotion
Swarmed in the seas and grew, diversified
And reproduced abundantly and multiplied

And to these fresh formed lands, after awhile
A coconut would float onto the shores
Adrift for who knows how many a mile
A bird would drop some seeds, mushrooms their spores
(Some spores survive millennia in style
In outer space, tiny ambassadors
That came to earth back in the distant past
Bearing a gift to man of visions unsurpassed)

The coconut will sprout; seeds germinate
The roots will find themselves a spot of soil
Where rain and storm made rock disintegrate
And soon in many places vines will coil
And birds and insects help to fecundate
And if somehow we don't discover oil
And desecrate the place with every known device
We'll have a blossoming new tropic Paradise

We know that life can colonize a rock
That sprung up yesterday in the salt sea
It takes no time at all because a flock
Of life forms are already running free
It took a little longer on the cosmic clock
Because we had to start from scratch, you see
Back then when earth was forming as a planet
And oceans cooling off upon this hunk of granite

In every case incipient life arises
Wherever there's the possibility
Its forms are multitudinous, all shapes and sizes
Each one a master of adaptability
What doesn't work, life force devitalizes
Or gives the form a new ability
Lets it evolve a horn or tail, a new defense
Like hibernation, camouflage, great strength, intelligence

For life to thrive upon a barren land
Somewhere out in the middle of the sea
Upon a planet where life forms expand
Wherever there's an opportunity
Is really not so hard to understand
But what about the deeper mystery?
How did that life-transferring spark appear
Billions of years ago on earth's forbidding sphere?

Perhaps, by chance, a falling meteor hit
The earth, exploding like a hurricane
And carried elements of life with it
That spread upon that vast and stark terrain
Or possibly a stroke of lightning lit
The spark of life that started off the chain
Of living forms, that reaches to the present
Evolving shapes grotesque, strange and lovely, pleasant

Or could it be the merest accident
That out of nothing, up sprung living things?
Or did some creature that's omnipotent
Some master scientist control the strings
Using our world as an experiment
So he could watch our daily sufferings
And turn it to an interplanetary zoo
Where we are housed and fed and dream that it's all true?

I like the way that Michelangelo
Shows God and Adam on the Sistine ceiling
In a magnificent adagio
(Restored after five centuries of peeling)
They stretch their arms and through their fingers flow
(The painter, his great power and art revealing)
The gift of life, which God instilled in Adam
And then God played an encore by cloning Adam's madam

I see a vision of an ancient time
Upon a hill, above a stretch of sand
A figure that's unutterably sublime
A God from Michelangelo's own hand
Is gazing at the sky; I hear bells chime
I see Him wave His arms in gestures grand
And everything in the vicinity
Dissolves and opens up into infinity

We look out at a bowl of space that's boundless
There is no map, no sign, there's no direction
No movement, all is absolutely soundless
A face of darkness is its sole complexion
No shape, no sides, no top, no bottom, groundless
An empty canvas with no imperfection
Extensive distances so uncomputable
Untold, far-flung and fathomless, inscrutable

This God, This Absolute, This Soul Supreme
This Zeus, This Blessed One declares a gala
Jehovah, Brahma, Ra, This Living Dream
From Paradise, Elysium, Valhalla
The Way, The Word, The One, The All, The Beam
This Spirit Great, First Cause, Prime Mover, Allah
This Being Infinite, Creator, Force
This Eternal, Universal, This Almighty Source

This Immanence raises His hands and claps
He focuses the power of His will
There is a pause, a tiny time elapse
A hundred billion galaxies begin to fill
The universe; the night takes off her wraps
A hundred trillion flaming stars now spill
Epiphanies of light, which clearly trace
Their golden orbits on the loom of empty space

He has created life that's so intense
Some stars will burn ten billion years or more
Producing light and heat that is immense
Out of the living furnace of their fiery core
Enough to blur, confound the human sense
To blaze a trail, a starry corridor
Through the immensities of outer space
Which will, the never-ending darkness, now replace

These suns, these stars, created with a clap
By The Immortal One are not themselves immortal
Or did He bring them forth with just a finger snap
And while He did so, did I hear Him chortle?
And afterwards, I swear He took a nap
After creating this star-studded portal
And not because He needed a good rest
But just to contemplate what He made manifest

These living incandescences of light
Have generations like the human race
They live; they die, they're always burning bright
Some so aglow, that they burn out apace
From cosmic dust, debris, new stars ignite
Are born; red dwarfs, blue giants, double stars that grace
The vast empyrean. Are they immortal? No
They only live for eight, ten billion years or so

And then I saw The Everlasting brush
His hands across the sky; make time advance
Saw many billion years ceaselessly rush
Ahead, the birth and death of stars, the cosmic dance
I saw black holes and super novas blush
As they exploded into radiance
And twinkling stars that seemed content and tame
Spout hundred mile geysers of phosphorescent flame

I saw the way the star beams, sun-rays touch
A wandering planet's cold virginity
And free it from that sterile icy clutch
And turn the light, the life, the energy
Of which The Source has given them so much
Into that splendid gift, fecundity
And radiate into the planet's womb
That vital spark of life that makes a dead world bloom

Yes, God is riding on the waves of light—
Not in the way Slim Pickens took his ride
In that great film called Doctor Strangelove, right?
Shouting yahoo, waving his cowboy hat, astride
A missile plunging into that good night
But in a way a bit more dignified
The Essence rides within the star, the starlight beam
And at the speed of light flows through the universal stream

I saw huge planets spinning round their sun
So close that everything was roaring fire
Yet life forms danced, transparent figures spun
In widening circles, leaping ever higher
It seemed they actually were having fun
But I was not so bold as to inquire
These planets sported gaping molten scars
And shone almost as bright as their own stars

There was a planet seemed a Paradise
Where strange exotic shapes and daring forms
Landscaped a perfect world of solid ice
That sparkled crystal clear between the storms
This architecture, noble and precise
Housed furry animals who crawled in swarms
Throughout the caves and palaces snow white
And carved and polished them under three large moon's light

Time flew; I saw the universe expand
The meteors and comets drifting by
Stars like a million beaches' grains of sand
Innumerable, no way to quantify
He had designed a living wonderland
Constructed it, and stuck it in the sky
A fruitful, self-engendering perfection
Which He, with twinkling eye, revealed for my inspection

The Master Potter brought into my view
New galaxies that danced upon the edge
Formed recently from spatial residue
So far, astronomers can but allege
That they exist. I visited a few
Amazing worlds. It was a privilege
To land upon the surface of these planets
As fresh and full of bursting life as pomegranates

Each tree and bush was rosy with the flush
Of fruit so soft and ripe, never would they harden
A mass of jungle foliage so plush
And elegant, you'd have to beg its pardon
With every step into the underbrush
Cascades and dripping fountains filled this garden
And creatures of all kinds and forms and shapes
Were heard and seen, as through the rolling hills they'd traipse

Some galaxies had many stars that held
A good few dozen planets in control
On most of which some sort of life forms dwelled
In fact, throughout the passage of the whole
Wide universe, trackless, unparalleled
I saw as many planets in the cosmic bowl
As I saw stars. Unless conditions were extreme
On almost the majority, life reigned supreme

Yes, life insists on rising everywhere
No scientist could be half as persuasive
With all his passé theories doctrinaire
Than my first-hand observing how pervasive
The life force is, once it takes hold, I swear
It is ubiquitous; on earth, at times, invasive
Like kudzu, morning glory and wisteria
Burn it, chop it, you can't stop it; it's like hysteria

We zoomed in on the system of our sun
I'd say, about two billion years ago
And looked at earth when life barely begun
A restless, surging, molten mass, aglow
And using my new microscopic vision
I saw protozoa wriggle and algae grow
Time passed; I watched the mountains form, sponges appear
In shallow seas, invertebrates, a biosphere

I saw the coral reefs grow and extend
And thought of the good ship Heraclitus
Of all the valiant efforts of many a friend
Who work for man and earth, to reunite us
To save the world, the sea, the reefs; amend
The wrongs, so earth can once again delight us
(Sierra, Kathelin, Thrity, Margaret, Fred); all strive
(Flash, Brad, Gaie, Laser, Johnny, Tango); to keep this world alive

I saw the scorpion appear on land
And scaly fish start swimming in the sea
Amphibians crawl out upon the sand
Massive, luxuriant growth of fern and tree
Reptilian life arise, quickly expand
And insects flit about in brilliancy
I watched the dinosaurs prepare for dominating
The world, and tiny mammals sitting tight and waiting

Waiting until they'd all be sitting pretty
As if they knew exactly what would happen
And dreamed, perhaps, of forming a committee
Once dinosaurs slipped up and were caught nappin'
Of living out their lives in a big city
Perhaps, their genes could hear the future tappin'
For soon an asteroid sent reptiles down the tube
By landing in what's now the town of Chicxulub

Where after sixty million years had passed
Sweet Linda of my heart brought forth a daughter
Whom we named for a princess of high-caste
The Maya Nicte-Ha, flower of the water
Perhaps, we should have named her for the blast
That had precipitated reptile slaughter
Or for the tiny mammals who possibly foresaw
This human birth upon the Yucatecan shore

I saw the stages of development
In plant and animal society
From a few forms to the magnificent
Array of multifaceted variety
I saw that animal of discontent
That beast of rampant impropriety
That poor, bare, forked, unhappy creature, man
Slowly evolve himself from the orangutan

And into every corner of the globe
He'd tramp and climb and crawl, explore and wander
In coves and caves he'd stick his nose and probe
Investigate, observe, remember, ponder
He'd sew a furry hide into a robe
And trek through ice and snow, forever yonder
Developing a range of flexibility
To deal with earth's appalling incivility

A myriad of generations passed
With man engaged in gathering and hunting
Until he freed himself (he thought) at last
From all the problems that he found confronting
His efforts to secure each day's repast
He learned to work the land and sweating, grunting
He'd till and sow and reap and store the grain
Not knowing he was forging links upon the chain

That binds a man who's free, makes him a slave
A slave bound to the earth from which he rose
Born free as bird and beast or wind and wave
And now entrammeled by the path he chose
Trading the freedom The Creator gave
So he could press a grindstone to his nose
Trading his independence for a steady meal
And thinking that he got the best end of the deal

With agriculture 'twas an easy jump
From farm to hamlet, village, sprawling town
Then cities rising from what was a clump
Of shires, cantons, provinces clustered round
Grew into empires, huge and swollen, plump
With colonies belonging to the crown
Where lords and ladies dined and interbred
And common folk worked day and night to see them fed

And man increased in number, quickly grew
Hacked out a home on every continent
It was a feat to clear an acre or two
Although it barely even made a dent
On mighty forests reaching to the blue
Then in a flash, before he could repent
The simple axe he swung became a power saw
That turned the forests, jungles into sticks of straw

It was no easy trick to catch a fish
Or run a deer down in the bush or plain
Man had to struggle hard to get a dish
Of tasty food, and often toiled in vain
If only things were easier, he'd wish
If only he could ride the pleasure train
Then oceans were fished out, whales gone, in just a blink
And species everywhere, on land and sea, extinct

The breathing apparatus of the world
That pumps the breath of life and thus maintains us
These jungles of the tropic zones unfurled
Also produce the magic potion that unchains us
From all the maladies that Nature's hurled
Upon our heads, that hobble and constrain us
And yet we amputate our lungs, the cures erase
We're cutting off our noses just to spite our face

Macadam ribbons squeeze the earth as tight
As ropes around a man tied to the stake
A billion vehicles race day and night
Upon these roads, this all constricting snake
To satisfy the engine's appetite
We drill for oil constantly, their thirst to slake
And feed it to them all the time and everywhere
For thanks, they roar and belch black smoke into the air

We pour our waste upon the land, in river, sea
Great stacks shoot poison gas ten miles high
Streams filled with chemicals burn constantly
We've torn a gaping hole in the sky
We've polished and improved the recipe
To blow the world apart easy as pie
With alcohol, tobacco, we've been conscienceless
But firmly outlaw what expands the consciousness

Our future's thirty years of mortgage payments
So many hundred dollars every month
Of running from a couple dozen claimants
Whose attitude and tactics are quite blunt
Of paying off your charge card for the raiments
You bought your ex-wife to maintain her front
Of honky-tonks and everything that's phony
Of raising some quick cash for her damn alimony

Of wondering why you've got so much insurance
Because you need to die or sicken to collect
You bet against yourself; take my assurance
But then there's nothing much to lose but self-respect
Of hoping you've the strength and the endurance
And one more signature to write another check
Make sure it doesn't bounce or their computer
Will clean you out as thoroughly as roto-rooter

Each time you buy commodities or stocks
And place your money in the futures market
The chances are you're going to lose your socks
Don't speculate, they warn, but do you mark it?
You worry how the future, cunning fox
Will treat your car, every time you park it
When you return will it be smashed beyond repair
Or lucky enough to find that it's no longer there?

We have exchanged our freedom and our joy
To live our lives inside a tiny box
The earth, we have consented to destroy
To own a car, a TV set, a door that locks
We sacrifice the world to buy a toy
And are the interplanetary laughing-stocks
We have wiped out most every trace of natural man
Who was this planet's partner and its custodian

The coral reef is waving us good-bye
Its polyps clogged with sewage dumped off shore
And tears of mercury fall from the fish's eye
The fields of grain beg us to spray no more
We hear the forests groan this lullaby:
"Who was supposed to be minding the store?"
I noticed that The Grand Designer looked a little glum
And I implored Him to reveal what is to come

He showed a number of scenarios
In one, an asteroid hit the equator
And earth collapsed like falling dominos
Went down in flames just like an aviator
Another one had generalissimos
Press buttons on their pet disintegrator
The general effect was like the first
In both these instances the planet simply burst

In one, madmen and cancer cells, disease
Had overrun the world and gone amuck
The deadly virus spread on every passing breeze
And left men sick or dead or terror-struck
I hoped there were some other possibilities
Or earth had run completely out of luck
One future variant gave earth a decent chance
If animals stepped down and gave control to plants

This sounded good. The Source strode off in space
I was alone and thought of Keats' utterance:
"...When I behold upon the night's starred face
Huge, cloudy symbols of a high romance
And think that I may never live to trace
Their shadows with the magic hand of chance..."
I'd seen The God unroll His universal scheme —
Like Keats, I cried: " ...Was it a vision or a waking dream..."

I've always felt the kingdom of the plants
Was higher on the evolutionary scale
Than man, whose discontent and arrogance
Makes most of his grand efforts doomed to fail
Least comfortable of all earth's occupants
Instead of learning from, he kills the whale
The forests that he needs; and is so maladroit
On land and sea, rather than harvest, he'll exploit

Plant life is so complete, so self-contained
It is not driven on by raw emotion
It does not, all the time, need to be entertained
In place it dances, free from locomotion
It does not hunt or kill, is self-sustained
Turning the sun and rain into a potion
That courses through its veins as green as jade
And turns the mind "...to a green thought in a green shade..."

The roots of plants under the planet's floor
All touch and twist and curl, communicate
A web beneath the land, from shore to shore
Where information, feelings circulate
They hold the earth together; don't make war
They grow and bloom and fruit and softly fecundate
The driving force within the green fuse flows
Plants intertwine, but don't step on each other's toes

Plants have already found the perfect way
To put the animals to work for them
Providing fruit and nectar night and day
And this enticing, gentle stratagem
Has mammals, reptiles, insects, birds repay
Their hosts for tasting their sweet diadem
By spreading seeds around; and on their wings or fur
Bring precious loads of pollen dust from him to her

And man himself is in the plants' employ
Keeping the wave of green always alive
Planting from Timbuktu to Illinois
And waiting for the harvest to arrive
The fruits of all his labor to enjoy
Man's one more beast who helps the plants to thrive
We animals are just a work force plants enlist
While animals without the plants, could not exist

A man once dug a hole in his yard
And planted himself in it to the thighs
He got his wife to water him and guard
His body till he could acclimatize
He hoped his human nature to discard
Become a tree of monumental size
I don't remember how the story ended
But always thought this man's idea was truly splendid

When I pass on please lay me in the ground
No coffin, just a winding sheet or shroud
And plant a long-lived redwood on the mound
That will be watered by the thundercloud
And through the centuries my essence will abound
Within its root and bark and leaf and trunk unbowed
And this will be my bid for immortality
Embodied in the wood, the heartwood of a tree.

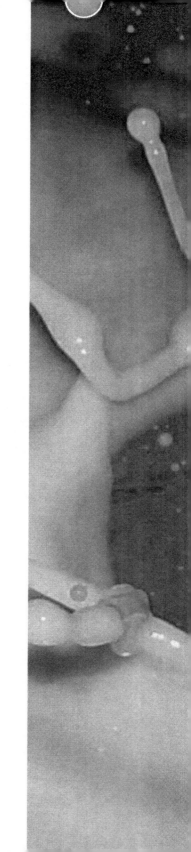

canto eight

DREAMS

There's rosy fingered dawn sweeping the sky
Whisking away the night's dark residue
And through the foggy windowpane I spy
Some blushing clouds suffused in coral hue
Unfold themselves as they go floating by
Like pillowed feather beds waving adieu
I blink and hide my head under the cover
Then leap up into day like an eager lover

My mind is foggy as the windowpane
A splash of icy water does the trick
I throw some clothes around my bodily domain
Like any other normal lunatic
Three brush strokes for the hair above my brain
So, straight up in the air it doesn't stick
And feeling fit as a middleweight contender
I shuffle to the kitchen where I grab the blender

And pour into it milk of rice, Rice Dream
And half as much again apricot nectar
Some psyllium and protein meal supreme
And ground up seeds and nuts just to perfect her
Then whip it up until it flows like cream
The drink of gods, this wondrous resurrecter
And that is how I make my daily déjeuner
And then I have another giant glass five times a day

Now that I'm fortified sipping my shake
I slip into a chair facing the east
And let the dawn upon my body break
The rising sun leaps like a fiery beast
Above the mountain tops and starts to bake
My blood and bones until I feel released
From the chill that permeates the morning air
And melt under the sun's delicious, friendly glare

Mornings are cold in old New Mexico
Even in the dog days of the summer
Up in my cozy mountain top chateau
And during winter you can wake up number
Than the frozen fingers of an Eskimo
Which, to use the colloquial, is a bummer
But when the blazing summer sun is so oppressing
Those chilly, early morns are welcomed as a blessing

Today I see the birds of spring arriving
A robin sits atop a piñon tree
A hummingbird is practicing his diving
And all the winter stay-at-homes, the chickadee
The finches, titmice, wrens are all contriving
To find seeds on the ground that I can't see
The jay, of course, the raven and the first magpie
Are darting, flapping, soaring across the azure sky

I wish that I could fly on feathered wings
And feel the rapid heartbeat in my breast
To soar and glide like birds or fairy kings
Of feathered or of gossamer wings possessed
And span the oceans in my voyagings
And float aloft forever without rest
Circle the world from pole to pole, around, across
With just a stroke or two like the mighty albatross

Who crosses oceans like we cross the street
Lives on the cutting edge, the avant-guard
And in himself is totally complete
Who knows the open sea as his backyard
And while we pace the continent's concrete
He sails above the watery boulevard
This long-winged, hook-beaked, invincible explorer
Bursting through the waves of his own brilliant aura

We soar in dreams as on the wings of love
Transported in the twinkling of an eye
To realms and provinces beyond, above
And flying crooked like the butterfly
We flit about until a call or shove
Awakes us from this dreamy lullaby
And clips the wings of insubstantiality
And drops us down again into reality

Our souls take flight within the sea of dreams
That packed-with-action magic picture show
Where life's not what it is, but what it seems
Staged by an unknown impresario
Presenting the mind's eye with rare extremes
Of images from bliss to vertigo
More than just images, we feel a true despair
Or joy; we are the actors in our own nightmare

More real than movies where we sit and watch
Screen idols smile and play the perfect part
With movie mouths of teeth without a splotch
Where everyone's a princess or a tart
More real than life's dull niche or dreary notch
More poignant, real, as beautiful as art
Movies and dance and song are man's evocative
Salt-sweet cry-in-the-night attempt to make dreams live

A fancy floats into the mind of man
A thought, a wish, what we might call a dream
The rumbling beginnings of a plan
The first, faint flickering of light, a gleam
An urge, an appetite, a need to span
The whole of an all-encompassing theme
And turn this vague idea, this intuition
This germ, this seed into magnificent fruition

And up springs art in forms so various
To wake the senses is why we create
So we can apprehend the glorious
And stir our hearts and souls to mitigate
The dark influence of the fatuous
It's life and love and dreams we celebrate
Despite the endless trivia we have to juggle
It's death, what's after death, and during life, the struggle

A dream's a lot like going to the theatre
You take a seat, get comfortable, relax
Or go to bed, to sleep, try not to stir
Forget about life's ordinary facts
You're in the dark, don't know what will occur
The show begins, proceeds, reaches climax
You're moved, you're bored, you're thrilled; it's great, it's rotten
You leave, or you wake up, and most of it's forgotten

But sometimes the experience is deep
Like Dead of Night, Children of Paradise
The stage or screen can make your soul leap
And fasten your attention like a vise
Shakespeare and Sophocles will make you weep
As, the spirit from the body, they entice
Theatres of dreams and dreams themselves can be daunting
Whose whole and shattered images we find so haunting

The play, the flick, the dream may turn out bad
We can leave the theatre, from dreams wake up
Ask for our money back, were we not clad
In our pajamas, sleepy, without make up
But, seriously, at whom can we get mad
For dreams that leave us feeling like we'll break up?
At what director or producer can we scream?
Who is responsible for this appalling dream?

"...The nightmare rides upon sleep..." Yeats once said
Talking about bad times in Ireland
And would say more, I'm sure, were he not dead
Words were completely under his command
The nightmare's hooves may prance through any bed
Her shining flanks wet from the Rio Grande
Her nostrils snorting flame, her shadow silhouette
A rush of wind and you awake half drowned in sweat

And Hamlet said: "...Good God, I could be bounded
In a nutshell and still count myself king
Of infinite space..." thus Hamlet expounded
"...Were it not that I have bad dreams..." a string
Of pearls, these fine words, which left me astounded
The first time that I heard their uttering
So powerful were the effects of his bad dreams
As the tailor said: the mend justifies the seams

A daydream and a night dream are similar
A million images slowly unwind
From the pedestrian to the bizarre
A reel of pictures, scattered, intertwined
The only difference is, by day you are
The prime projectionist; the conscious mind
Controls everything played on your inner screen
In sleep, subconscious mind is running the machine

Is all our world the dream of some great God
Who's catching forty winks between affairs
On distant worlds where only Gods have trod
Who's trying to forget his godly cares
And drifted off into the land of Nod
Taking a nap upon the crystal stairs
That spiral up into those gorgeous cloud-capped towers?
Is every dreaming wink of his a million years of ours?

I slept and dreamt I was a butterfly
And woke not knowing if I was a man
Who sleeping, dreamed he was a butterfly
Or butterfly who dreamed he was a man
This story was designed to testify
To facts well known in days when time began
The waking world and world of dreams, both equal, real
Are just two different spokes that turn on the same wheel

Sometimes I wake up in the morning to
A world I'm sure I've never seen before
Where animals grow roots and plants are blue
And on my pillow there's a little door
That widens as I start in climbing through
And then I'm talking with the Emperor
And hear the barking, barking of the royal pup
And wake, to find I dreamed that I had woken up

One day I woke remembering a friend
Whom I'd not seen at all for many a year
Who wrote that he was going to extend
A trip to the west coast and visit here
I looked through letters for the one he penned
So I could get the date exactly clear
The thought of seeing him again had me beaming
Till I realized he was long dead and I'd been dreaming

There lived in Baghdad once a wealthy man
And made of money, who lost all he had
He slaved each day aboard a moving van
One night he fell asleep in his rags clad
And in a dream he saw a holy man
Who said, "Thy fortune is in Cairo" and he bade
The ruined man go thither, from his house to slip
Into the night and straightway start upon that trip

So he set out for Cairo, and arriving
As evening fell, found shelter in a mosque
Where, while he slept, by Allah's strange contriving
A band of bandits entered from the bosk
And made their way, these masters of conniving
To an adjoining house with a kiosk
The owners wakened by the noise of thieves cried out
And soon police appeared in answer to their shout

The robbers had made off, but then the Chief
On entering the mosque found the man sleeping
And mad, not having caught a single thief
Began to beat the man with palm rods, heaping
Blow after blow on him without relief
Until the man, half-dead, at last stopped weeping
They cast him into jail, broken, melancholy
For three whole days, till sent for by the Chief, the Wali

"Where are you from?" the Wali asked of him
"From Baghdad have I come" the man replied
"What brought thee here to Cairo, was it a whim?"
"I saw one in a dream," the man from Baghdad sighed
"Who told me I should spare not life nor limb
But rise right up and off to Cairo ride
And find my fortune here; but what he promised me
Proved naught but palm rod beatings which I got from thee"

The Wali laughed showing his wisdom teeth
"O man of little wit, thrice have I seen
In dreams, one who a fortune would bequeath
Who said, in Baghdad is a house, pale green
In such a place, of such a type; beneath
A garden courtyard stands a mezzanine
And at the lower end where you can see the mountain
A climbing rose cascades around a jetting fountain"

"Right there is buried a great sum of gold
Go thither and take it. Yet I went not!
But thou, of such brief wit, have made so bold
On the faith of a dream to journey to this spot"
The Wali gave him some money to help hold
The man together on his homeward trot
Now the house the Wali had described was the man's own
House in Baghdad; and after a long journey home

The wayfarer arrived, dug in the earth
Beside the fountain, thinking what a pleasure
It was returning to his land of birth
And soon turned up a monumental treasure
Filling a casket of enormous girth
And Allah granted him a life of leisure
The Thousand And One Nights titles this tale supreme
The Ruined Man Who Became Rich Again Through A Dream

I think it's time to have another shake
To set me up, to get me through the day
To soothe the dull and dreadful inner ache
Insisting that I feed the mortal clay
Disdaining bread, I cry: let me drink cake!
I have become a true liquid gourmet
My dining pleasure now revolves around the blender
Drinking these concentrated essences of splendor

It seems a shame; to live others must die
That we must kill the beast, the bird, the fish
To feed our flesh, their flesh we mortify
We see them only as a tasty dish
Not sentient beings just like you and I
Who feel and pulse with life; sometimes I wish
We carnivores would start out one day bright and sunny
To only feed on foods of life like milk and honey

Man cannot live, they say, by bread alone
He needs to breathe the life instilling air
To smell the breeze that wafts nature's cologne
To thrill, vibrate, to touch and be aware
To hear the ringing of the telephone
To let him know that he is really there
To work and think, converse and play, take deep draughts of
The cooling waters of life's well, to laugh and love

'...To sleep: perchance to dream: aye, there's the rub
For in that sleep of death what dreams may come..."
Brought by the unknown guest or Beelzebub
That will delight us or will leave us numb
Or do the members of Death's lofty club
To drifting fantasies and dreams succumb?
"...We are such stuff as dreams are made on, and our little
Life is rounded with a sleep..." so fragile and so brittle

The deep investigations of Marquis
D'Hervey de Saint-Denis concerning dreams
Who wrote back in the nineteenth century
Begins with the development, it seems
And cultivation of oneiric memory
Which will improve under certain regimes
And after some six months of special training
He could remember all the dreams he was entertaining

And then, proceeding from the principle
That neither the attention nor the will
Are lost in sleep, but are accessible
He focused all his energy and skill
On what is thought to be quite inconceivable:
Controlling his own dreams; now don't get ill
He had success in doing so, to an extent
Endowed with special aptitudes for this experiment

But at the cost of efforts so immense
And under such a rigid discipline
Not likely to encourage other gents
To follow on the path that he walked in
I hope I'm giving you a certain sense
Of this strange chap; 'cause I'm still trying to pin
Him down, to find his books, his work to understand
Right now, most everything I've got is second-hand

But what a perfect second hand we've got!
I've learned about d'Hervey from Maurice Maeterlinck
Whose sparkling prose sails like a racing yacht
On troubled seas of philosophic ink
Whose clear, incisive style hits the spot
Like an oasis on the desert's brink
He talks of principles on which, the majority
Of oneirologists, strangely enough, agree

The first is that there is no dreamless sleep
It is impossible the brain should cease
Completely functioning however deep
We doze; the liver, kidneys still release
Toxins, stomach digests, lungs breathe, hearts beat
D'Hervey assured himself of this, so says Maurice
By being constantly wakened throughout his nightly scrimmage
And always found his thoughts were fixed on an oneiric image

The second principle admits that we
Can cultivate, develop (like we do
The ordinary waking memory)
The dreaming or oneiric memory too
The simplest method is to simply
Make written notes on each dream passing through
As soon as we're awakened by the morning light
And every time that we wake up during the night

After a while our memories begin
To lend themselves to the new regimen
And with the practice of this discipline
We learn to reconstruct our dreams, amen
And odd as it must seem, as though they've been
Flattered by the honor we are paying them
Our dreams become less incoherent, more regular
Like children, knowing they are watched, on their best behavior

Dreams are the product of an organ which
During the waking state's under control
And tuned exclusively to Reason's pitch
In sleep this organ's independent role
Is manifest; it wanders through the rich
Illimitable universal soul
And drops the foolish notion of those twin illusions
Space and Time, which mask eternal present, in confusions

It's noon — I'll try a walk around the garden
Spring bulbs are popping out their flowery heads
I almost stepped on one; I beg your pardon
They won't stand still for staying in their beds
I warn them but they're used to disregardin'
Most everything I say; a bulb just spreads
Until you're walking on a carpet made of flowers
Whose woof and warp's so fragrant that it overpowers

Sometimes I dream I'm dancing with the flowers
Their willow slimness folded in my arms
We whirl about in summer thundershowers
Their leaves, caressing gently, fill my palms
And I might steal a kiss beneath the bowers
And they kiss back without the slightest qualms
Their petals with exquisite softness brush my lips
And we embrace as pollen flies and nectar drips

If I could find a plant who'd take a chance
I know I'm ready and extremely willing
If there arose the proper circumstance
I think there's nothing that could be more thrilling
Than honeymooning in the south of France
To intertwine, our essences distilling
To love and bring forth a brand new kind of creature
Superior to man and plant in every feature

I won't commit an impropriety
By talking of the actual mechanics
Creating a new species or variety
Is not a case of sexual botanics
But more a form of sacred inebriety
A mix of tenderness and sheer volcanics
A tipsy, cosmic rush of spinning vertigo
That turns a dream—into a living embryo

So, I was strolling in the garden when
A vivid black and yellow butterfly
Flew lazy circles round my head and then
He fluttered off into the limpid sky
And suddenly he reappeared again
Which somehow got me started wondering why
No one has yet devised a simple working scheme
For capturing the sounds and pictures of a dream

Some variation of a VCR
A threadlike wire that we could attach
Before we sleep, upon the jugular
Or on the head, the eye lid, with a patch
If we can get a signal from a star
It should be elementary to catch
Our dreams, as they go passing through our teeming brain
On tape or disc, and all their images retain

This is a cry: Let scientists get cracking!
Inventors, wake! And hurry to the bench
What we have is a serious something lacking
Some principle we call on you to wrench
From out those muffled layers of dense packing
Those cobwebs in the brain. Arise and quench
Our thirst with an invention that will stop my screams
And let the conscious mind fathom the world of dreams

Which is a world akin to depths of ocean
Where from the surface nothing much is seen
Distorted by an undulating motion
As through a window streaked with kerosene
So one is left without the foggiest notion
Of what occurs beneath that rippling screen
And then with just a snorkel, mask and pair of fins
A fuller understanding, of what's below, begins

To spur us to a further exploration
Conceive, design the necessary tools
Refine our vessels for the navigation
Of all the ocean's deepest, darkest pools
And if we concentrate on preservation
Constraining all the vandals and the fools
We'll open a new world and while enjoying it
We'll learn from its life forms without destroying it

We are aware that dreams have their own world
But we're unconscious of the great effect
They'd have (if all their secrets were unfurled)
Upon our lives by helping us perfect
The way we deal with curves that Fate has hurled
So valuable are things that we neglect—
Follow your dream, even to the utmost measure
And like the man from Baghdad, you will find your treasure

There is a subject I'm investigating
Which is a special state of dreaming where
The dreamer, into the dream goes penetrating
To a degree that makes him so aware
And conscious of the dream that he's creating
That he can change or stop it in mid-air
They call it lucid dreaming and I have no doubt
It's like what d'Hervey's dream control is all about

I'm sure that you remember friend d'Hervey
Of dreams, the monumental pioneer
Whose books seem to have all but slipped away
Only five libraries on the entire sphere
Have copies of Les Rêves, or so they say
The good news is, before they disappear
The French came out with all of d'Hervey recently
And want translators for poor monoglots like me

Who has at his disposal but one tongue
Of all the languages you might collect
With which this universal frame is strung
And limps like a disabled architect
Who slowly climbs a ladder with one rung
And tries to cover up this grave defect
But I can double talk in French, appearing suave
And in my dreams I speak Urdu and fluent Slav

I wonder if it's possible to learn
A foreign language while you're fast asleep?
I know the playing of a tape can burn
Some words into your brain while counting sheep
But I would like to wake from my sojourn
My nightly passage through the dreamy deep
Having another language under my command
That I, and natives of that tongue can understand

I'd also like, on opening my eyes
To find that all my best dreams have come true
A world of whipped cream heaped on apple pies
And every bite as sweet as honeydew
Where all the songs are soft as lullabies
Under a canopy of lucky blue
With ease and plenty, cakes and ale, delicious mirth
But then, of course, we'd be in Heaven not on Earth

Is it the dream of Heaven that can pull
(Over the eyes of several billion souls)
That legendary and proverbial wool
So he who offers up that dream controls
These untold legions of the worshipful
And lists them permanently on his rolls?
Does this sustain the kamikaze; build Valhalla?
Is this dream the eternal Paradise of Allah?

I dreamed that I possessed a magic wand
And with it could perform heroic feats
I'd turn a drab brunette into a blond
And dinners that I threw, into Dutch treats
Make those who didn't like me, over fond
Change little rooms into one-bedroom suites
But nothing satisfied; it didn't seem heroic
To merely make a dark haired woman xanthochroic

So instantly I took another tack
With miracles a little more dramatic
Made half the world, the other half, attack
Turned every moderate to a fanatic
I rearranged the starry zodiac
Transformed Caucasian into Asiatic
These wonders I performed, these things unprecedented
Which only turned unsatisfied into discontented

I split the wand in half lengthwise and then
Like the broom of the sorcerer's apprentice
It multiplied over and over again
I threw them all over a precipice
So that the race of able bodied men
Now had a magic wand, and every Miss
And Ms. and Mrs., all had the enormous power
To change the world, create, destroy, enrich, devour

I woke and found this dream a little puzzling
Then realized passing out the wands was right
Mankind already has (no need for muzzling)
The power to tear apart or to unite
But now, if you'll excuse, it's time for guzzling
Another shake, before day turns to night
I pour the first drops on the earth as a libation
To the Muse, the Goddess of my imagination

I wonder if two people made a pact
That each would dream about the other one
And in their dreams they'd meet somewhere, in fact
Their dreams would simultaneously run
And they would always meet in the exact
Same spot, and after years and decades spun
When Death enveloped one or both in his embrace
Would they still meet in dreams at the same time, same place?

When I go to sleep I never count sheep
I count all the charms about Linda
And lately it seems in all of my dreams
I walk with my arms about Linda
And when I awake it's coffee and cake
And I'm singing psalms about Linda
And this melody is no mystery
I just hope that she dreams sweet dreams about me

The source, the fountainhead whence springs all art
All music, dance, all creativity
All dreams, of course; is something quite apart
From the intelligence, whose guarantee
Is that it keeps the horse behind the cart
Lets reason stop the ever flowing sea
Of inspiration from the universal soul
Before it reaches conscious mind's complete control

Intelligence evolved a wall of steel
Its own version of the iron curtain
To keep reason alive it needs conceal
All random images of the uncertain
To think (it thinks) is better than to feel
Its time is spent exclusively subvertin'
The flowing primal stream that it has marked taboo
And we must drink the tiny sips of what leaks through

If we could cut a channel in the gate
So that our dreams we'd perfectly remember
But carefully, so we don't alienate
The mind, and turn ourselves into a member
Of that strange club where brains are a blank slate
If we could tunnel through, and watch that ember
Become a flame of pure volcanic energy
What lava flows of revelations we might see!

I think this is the proper place to mention
That if the gates swung wide and dreams burst through
We'd all be working on some new invention
Creating things is all we'd ever do
There'd be a passage from the fifth dimension
Straight to the consciousness of me and you
As he who lately held the whole world in his palm
Was well aware; the little general, young Tom

To get in touch with that which in you flows
Beneath the threshold of the conscious mind
To be enveloped in the force that knows
The primal urge of earliest mankind
Is to step up from outer porticos
Into the inner sanctum and to find
What was before a faint and fleeting intimation
Of distant music — is now a full blown orchestration

O what parades, what cause to celebrate
To be there when the saints come marching in
O what a day when we tear down the gate
And learn the secrets of our origin
To meet that long invisible shipmate
To look into each other's eyes and grin
To hear, in full, what were mere hints of the compelling
Unfathomed universal tale that he's been telling

"I have a dream," said Martin Luther King
"Good night, sweet dreams," is what our loved ones say
"May all your dreams come true," says everything
My mother asked, "Why do you dream all day?"
A dream within a dream is comforting
When dreaming, don't let life get in the way
In sleeping visions great ideas rise up like cream
Tartini composed the Devil's Sonata in a dream

Sam Coleridge had a dream in which he saw
A mighty poem unroll before his eyes
Some several hundred lines or maybe more
He later said that he could visualize
Those images and rhymes without a flaw
The poem's beauty, quality and size
Upon awakening he could remember all
And putting pen to paper he began to scrawl

The lines, "In Xanadu did Kubla Khan
A stately pleasure dome decree
Where Alph, the sacred river ran…"
And in this eager writing reverie
He wrote some fifty lines until a man
From Porlock, on some business came to see
Coleridge, who after more than a good hour's delay
Found that the vision had completely passed away

Like images you see upon the surface
Of pools wherein a pebble has been thrown
All shattered, broken up, dissolved, amiss
His vision had in spreading circles flown
Like half forgotten memories of a kiss
And those few lines he penned now stood alone
Yet from dim recollections still in his cranium
He hoped one day to finish; that day has never come

So I implore you, friends, until the day
Invention's mother, dull Necessity
Has dragged one of her offspring from his play
To work at making a facsimile
Machine for dreams, which otherwise decay
Within our weak oneiric memory
I say, my friends, write down your dreams right on the spot
A moment later and they all will be forgot

There are some dreams, which constantly recur
Some nightmares that you wish you could forget
That stick inside your mind, a prickly burr
And pose, for peaceful slumber, a real threat
Like a persistent, phantom torturer
Perched on your pillow with a bayonet
Take heart, the craft of lucid dreaming has evolved
Techniques with which this sort of problem can be solved

When you're asleep, and conscious of the fact
That you are in a dream, and no mistake
And quite aware that every single act
Which you perform, and of which you partake
What seems unreal or real or seems abstract
Is all a dream, you have the power to wake
At any time you wish, as often as you please
Or change the circumstance, or make the action freeze

Of course it takes some practice to refine
These new techniques, find what works best for you
So waking state and dreaming state align
There're several things you have to learn to do
And motivation is the bottom line
And regularity and patience too
If explorations of this unknown and uncharted
World are up your alley, I can get you started

Just pack up all your money in a box
And take the next plane out to Santa Fe
Make sure you get here by the equinox
And bring your work clothes and a résumé
I have the key to open all the locks
Of all the iron doors that block the way
We have a desert full of spirits, demons, devils
So come on out and join us in our nightly revels

Smohalla of the tribe of Nez Percé spoke thus:
"You shall not see my young men ever work
Who works, dreams not; and wisdom comes to us
In dreams. Plow the ground? Shall I take a dirk
And tear my mother's breast? Be serious
Dig for stone? Shall I dig under her skin and jerk
Away her bones? You say, cut grass, make hay. How dare
I even think to cut and sell my mother's hair?"

And Enkidu poured out his heart to Gilgamesh:
"Last night I dreamed again, my friend; the heavens moaned
An awful being sunk his claws into my flesh
And smothered me as I stood there alone
Transformed my arms to wings; caught in his mesh
I had no way of fighting him, I groaned
He led me to the place of darkest night, pitch black
Upon the road from which there is no coming back"

"There is the house whose people sit in darkness
Dust is their only food and clay their meat
They're clothed like birds with feathered wings for dress
Inside the house of dust, no light, no heat
I saw the kings of earth, now penniless
Who ruled in days of old when life was sweet
They, who stood in palaces and counted gods their kin
Stood now like slaves to fetch water from the water-skin"

"And in my dream, inside the house of dust
Were priests of incantation and of ecstasy
I saw the king of Kish, Etana the just
And Samuqan, the cattle god of high degree
Ereshkigal, queen of the underworld, august
And the recorder of the gods, Belit-Sheri
Who keeps the book of death; she held a tablet near
And seeing me she spoke, 'Who has brought this one here?' "

"Then I awoke like one who's drained of blood
Who wanders off alone into the waste
Like one the bailiff seized, heart pounding with a thud
My friend, when I into the earth am placed
O brother, when I'm set into the mud
Then let some god have my poor name erased
Or some great prince to guard your gate when I am dead
Let him obliterate my name and write his own instead"

And Gilgamesh heard all his words and wept
He listened to his friend and his tears flowed
He opened wide his mouth and the words crept:
"Your dream was marvelous; the terror a heavy load
But we treasure the dream, although it stepped
Upon the heart as if it would explode
For it has shown the end of life is sorrow supreme
Now I will pray, for my friend had an ominous dream"

I've started something autobiographic
O, not concerning my so-called real life
Which is humdrum, at times almost seraphic
Like an unrippled pool devoid of strife
But all about my dreams, their nightly traffic
Unlike my waking state, completely rife
With fantasy, weird episodes, embarrassments
Impossible escapes, mad schemes, bizarre events

A history of all the secret dreams
I've harbored in my heart and not revealed
Whose winding paths trace those recurrent themes
Of danger, struggle, triumph, wounds concealed
Adventures, escapades; a tale that teems
With flashing images bright as a shield
Of trust betrayed and friends forgot and faith renewed
Of lies and loyalty, good-will, ingratitude

Of dreams so secret even I don't know
Where they begin, what promenades they'll take
And all the scenes and episodes, which flow
In swirling images, coil like a snake
Around my waking memory also
And, do I dream or am I wide awake
Becomes a question that is always on my lips
Is it deep night or is the sun in an eclipse?

It seems to me invaluable to learn
The story of the life you live in sleep
For otherwise you may as well just burn
A third of all the memories you keep
Locked up, of each amazing night's sojourn
Into the world of dreams that's buried deep
Beneath your conscious mind. The story is exciting
And waiting to be told, if you can read the writing

Let's just suppose you suffered from amnesia
And sections of your memory were blocked
And nothing simple like milk of magnesia
Could open up connections that were locked
You'd seem to be under deep anesthesia
And always ready to go off half-cocked
There'd be a part of you unknown and obsolete
The story of your life unfinished, incomplete

Imagine having a split personality
Two different people there inside your skin
And each was unaware of the duality
Had no idea at all he was a twin
And that your field of speciality
Was publishing a daily bulletin
About the need to know thyself, the inner you
While deep inside, your twin lived there, and you never knew

I know a place where they have dreams for sale
A little shop along a busy street
They sell antiques; you see that coat of mail
So burnished that it throws off waves of heat
This figure here, an amber nightingale
These silken slippers made for tiny feet
There is a curtain at the far end of the store
Pass through, and on the left, a massive oaken door

Knock twice, then once, then twice again and wait
Kneel on the floor and tightly close your eyes
This is the sign; you'll hear a sliding grate
Hold very still until someone replies
By knocking back, and this will indicate
That now you have permission to arise
Enter, and find a warm and elegant venue
You'll be shown to an easy chair and given a menu

A list of dreams a thousand pages long
With twenty something dreams on every page
Dreams where you'll dance while bursting into song
Dreams where you'll live forever, never age
Dreams that will end up right, which started wrong
Dreams where you're tied and locked up in a cage
Dreams of suspense, adventure, flaming passion, magic
Historical, hysterical, comical and tragic

Select the dream that pleases you the most
Make changes in the script to suit your mood
Cast friends you'd like to honor or to roast
In parts you wish; choose tone and attitude
Switch sets into the mountains or the coast
Make cuts and rearrange, augment, exclude
It's not like hopping into town to see a flick
The filmmaker is you; it's you who choose and pick

And once you're satisfied with your selection
And take a mild sedative to lull
No drugs, hypnosis, there is no injection
A helmet's firmly placed upon your skull
And in a private room, after connection
You lean back and enjoy the spectacle
"What do they charge for this and what if I abhorred it?"
"If you have to ask what it costs, then you can't afford it"

This sets you free from all the random plots
The countless, winding, tortured, twisting ways
The symbols that obscure, the untied knots
The unexpected quagmires, the maze
The flaws, the gaps, the really scary spots
With which subconscious mind each night displays
For you, its own rendition of a solid dream
Now, you can buy a made to order one that is supreme

For certain folks this is a decent route
For those who find their dreams are always frightening
Jumping from planes without a parachute
Or constantly being hit by lightning
For those who think they never dream, as a substitute
For dark and boring nights that need some brightening
Bought dreams are fun, but have a slightly hollow ring
Compared to the pure majesty of the real thing

It is essential that you stay in tune
With all your dreams to live life at its peak
Subconscious mind is ready to commune
With you, and fashions dreams with which to speak
It wraps you every night in a cocoon
And whispers to you dancing cheek to cheek
And all that's necessary is that you remember
So you can blow into a flame, that dreaming ember

If I could visit you in darkest night
When you are fast asleep wrapped in your quilt
Bathed in a single ray of one star's light
That on your lips and cheeks so gently spilt
I'd walk into your dreams while you slept tight
And cover you with flowers that never wilt
And underneath the layers of your conscious mind
In your subconscious dreaming depths, uncoil, unwind

Bright day has closed the pages of her book
The faded sunset's just a memory
Dark night hangs from the curving ivory hook
The moon extends in her ascendancy
A million stars all beckon us to look
Beyond the confines of this galaxy
The melting snow pours down the mountainside in streams
Midnight—falling asleep—I'll see you in my dreams.

CPSIA information can be obtained at www.ICGtesting.com
Printed in the USA
LVOW101613070112

262612LV00004B/3/P